Letts

KS3

VISUAL REVISION GUIDE

SUCCESS

QUESTIONS & ANSWERS

QUESTIONS & ANSWERS

MATHEMATICS
Levels 5-8

Fiona Mapp

CONTENTS

Throughout the book, questions with a shaded panel behind their number are at level 8. 4

Homework Diary

TOPIC	SCORE
Numbers	/30
Positive and negative numbers	/32
Working with numbers	/29
Fractions	/33
Decimals	/36
Percentages 1	/31
Percentages 2	/32
Fractions, decimals, percentages and using a calculator	/33
Estimates and checking calculations	/35
Ratio	/27
Indices	/40
Standard index form	/36
Algebra 1	/35
Algebra 2	/34
Equations 1	/43
Equations 2 and inequalities	/36
Number patterns and sequences	/25
Coordinates and graphs	/17
More graphs	/26
Interpreting graphs	/16
Shapes	/28
Solids	/18
Symmetry	/24
Constructions and LOGO	/18
Angles and tessellations	/24
Bearings and scale drawings	/24
Transformations	/18
Loci and coordinates in 3D	/17
Pythagoras' Theorem	/25
Trigonometry in right-angled triangles	/28
Measures and measurement	/32
Similarity	/23
Area and perimeter of 2D shapes	/26
Volume of 3D solids	/23
Collecting data	/17
Representing data	/13
Scatter diagrams and misleading graphs	/16
Averages 1	/21
Averages 2	/17
Cumulative frequency graphs	/17
Probability 1	/19
Probability 2	/17

Progress Plotter

Once you have completed a unit, and filled in your score on the Homework Diary opposite, use this Progress Plotter to chart your success! Fill in the boxes with your score for each unit and watch your results get better and better.

	Nearly all right – excellent work!	*More than half –* good – but keep trying	*Less than half –* Room for improvement	*Under 5 –* needs more work
Numbers				
Positive and negative numbers				
Working with numbers				
Fractions				
Decimals				
Percentages 1				
Percentages 2				
Fractions, decimals, percentages and using a calculator				
Estimates and checking calculations				
Ratio				
Indices				
Standard index form				
Algebra 1				
Algebra 2				
Equations 1				
Equations 2 and inequalities				
Number patterns and sequences				
Coordinates and graphs				
More graphs				
Interpreting graphs				
Shapes				
Solids				
Symmetry				
Constructions and LOGO				
Angles and tessellations				
Bearings and scale drawings				
Transformations				
Loci and coordinates in 3D				
Pythagoras' Theorem				
Trigonometry in right-angled triangles				
Measures and measurement				
Similarity				
Area and perimeter of 2D shapes				
Volume of 3D solids				
Collecting data				
Representing data				
Scatter diagrams and misleading graphs				
Averages 1				
Averages 2				
Cumulative frequency graphs				
Probability 1				
Probability 2				

M Choose just one answer, a, b, c or d.

1 From this list of numbers: 4, 7, 9, 12, 20 which one is a prime number?
   a) 7 b) 4 c) 9 d) 20 (1 mark)

2 The positive square root of 64 is:
   a) 7 b) –8 c) –7 d) 8 (1 mark)

3 Work out the lowest common multiple of 6 and 8.
   a) 48 b) 3 c) 24 d) 2 (1 mark)

4 What is the value of 3^3?
   a) 9 b) 12 c) 72 d) 27 (1 mark)

5 What is the reciprocal of $\frac{7}{9}$?
   a) $\frac{9}{7}$ b) $\frac{7}{9}$ c) $\frac{9}{5}$ d) 9 (1 mark)

6 Calculate the highest common factor of 18 and 24.
   a) 6 b) 18 c) 12 d) 432 (1 mark)

Score .... /6

Q Answer all parts of all questions.

1 Some numbers are in the cloud.

12   6   1   13   49   17   27   4

From the cloud, write down the numbers which are:
   a) factors of 24 ....(1 mark)
   b) prime numbers........(1 mark)
   c) square numbers ....(1 mark)
   d) multiples of 6........(1 mark)

2 Here are some numbers:
   1, 3, 4, 5, 6, 8, 10, 12, 15, 20.
   Circle those numbers which are a factor of 30. ....(2 marks)

3 What is the LCM of 8 and 12? ....(1 mark)

4 What is the HCF of 14 and 40? ....(1 mark)

5 Write 60 as a product of its prime factors. ....(2 marks)

6 The reciprocal of $2\frac{1}{2}$ is $\frac{5}{2}$. True or false? ....(1 mark)

7 Write down all the factors of 24. ....(2 marks)

8 Write: a) 4 to the power of 3 .... b) 2 to the power of 5 .... (2 marks)

Score .... /15

S **These are SATs-style questions. Answer all parts of the questions.**

1 William has 12 counters. He can put them in 3 rows, with 4 counters in each row.

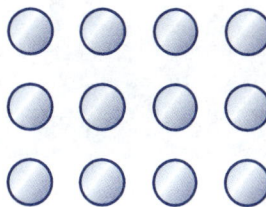

   a) Draw a diagram to show how he can put 12 counters in 2 rows, with the same number of counters in each row.

   (1 mark)

   b) Draw a diagram to show a different way that William can put 12 counters in a different number of rows, with the same number of counters in each row.

   (1 mark)

   c) Fill in the table to show how many rows William can make with 12 counters, and how many counters there are in each row.

Number of rows	Number of counters in each row
1 row	12 counters in each row
.... rows	.... counters in each row
3 rows	.... counters in each row
.... rows	.... counters in each row
.... rows	.... counters in each row
.... rows	1 counter in each row

   (4 marks)

   d) William says: *I can put 12 counters in 5 rows with the same number of counters in each row.*
   Explain why William is wrong. ....(1 mark)

2 Penelope and Tom are describing some numbers. Decide what numbers each is thinking about.
   Penelope *My number is a square number, greater than 10 and less than 20.*
   Tom   *My number is the only even prime number.*

   Penelope's number is...

   Tom's number is ....   (2 marks)

   Score .... /9

TOTAL SCORE   /30

For more help on this topic see KS3 Maths Success Guide pages 4–5

POSITIVE AND NEGATIVE NUMBERS

Q **Answer all parts of all questions.**

1 Here are some number cards: | 5 | –3 | 2 | –7 | 0 |

   a) Choose two cards that add up to give –10. ....(1 mark)

   b) Choose two cards that add up to give –7. ....(1 mark)

   c) Choose two cards that multiply to give –15. ....(1 mark)

2 Each of the calculations below has an answer which is one of the numbers from
   the list: 12, –12, –3, –4, 3, 8.
   Select the correct number for each answer.

   a) $-3 \times -4 =$ ....

   b) $-16 \div (-2) =$ ....

   c) $8 - (-4) =$ ....

   d) $4 + (-7) =$ ....

   e) $-9 \div (-3) =$ ....

   f) $-7 - (-3) =$ ....   (6 marks)

3 Work out the following.

   a) -7×-3 ....

   b) $-9 - (-4)$ ....

   c) $12 \div (-6)$ ....

   d) -8×2 ....   (4 marks)

4 The temperature at midday is –12°C. By midnight it has dropped a further 10°C. What
   is the temperature at midnight?

   ....(1 mark)

5 Here are some numbers in a number pyramid. The number in each rectangle is found by
   adding the two numbers below.
   Complete the number pyramid.

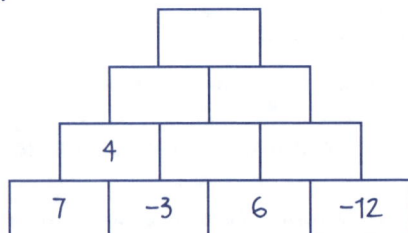

   | 7 | –3 | 6 | –12 |

   with 4 in the row above 7 and –3.

                                                        (2 marks)

6 Here are some signs: | + | × | ÷ | – |

   Insert the correct sign to make each calculation correct.

   a) -12 .... $-3 = 4$

   b) -7 .... $-3 = -4$

   c) 9 .... $-3 = -3$

   d) 12 .... $-5 = 7$ (4 marks)

Score .... /20

1 The arrow on the thermometer shows a temperature of 20°C.

°C
−10   0   10   20   30   40

↑
20°C

a) Draw an arrow on the thermometer to show a temperature of 32°C.
   Label the arrow 32°C.   (1 mark)

b) Draw an arrow on the thermometer to show a temperature of −7°C.   (2 marks)

c) The temperature was 25°C. It fell by 27°C.

   What is the temperature now? .... (1 mark)

d) The temperature was −9°C. It rose by 21°C.

   What is the temperature now? .... (1 mark)

e) Write these temperatures in order, hottest first.

   −6°C, 9°C, −3°C, 15°C, 0°C, −12°C

   ....°C, ...°C, ...°C, ...°C, ...°C, ...°C

   hottest   coldest   (1 mark)

2 Here is a list of numbers:

   −9, −5, −1, 0, 3, 2, 5

   Choose the number from the list to make each statement correct.

   a) $3 - \text{.............} = 4$ b) $5 \times \text{.............} = -25$

   c) $-9 + \text{.............} = -4$ d) $2 - \text{.............} = 7$

   e) $-9 \div \text{.............} = -3$ (5 marks)

   f) What is the total of all seven numbers in the list? ....(1 mark)

Score .... /12

TOTAL SCORE   /32

For more help on this topic see KS3 Maths Success Guide pages 6–7

Q **Answer all parts of all questions.**

1 You have four tins of beans with the weights written on them.

25 g	2250 g	2500 g	250 g
A	**B**	**C**	**D**

a) Write down the letters of two tins, where one tin is 100 times heavier than the other tin. ....(1 mark)

b) Which tin is 10 times heavier than a tin weighing 25 g? ....(1 mark)

2 Complete the magic square, so that each line of numbers along the horizontal, vertical and diagonal adds up to the same value.

6		8
	5	
2		

(2 marks)

3 Complete the following calculations, showing all your working.

a)   279
     42 x
    _____

b)   6305
     84 x
    _____

c)   37) 1665

d)   56) 4648

(4 marks)

4 A bar of chocolate costs 72 pence. How much would 37 bars cost? ....(1 mark)

5 A garden centre has 252 rose trees.
Each section of the garden centre has an equal number of rose trees.

If there are 6 sections, how many rose trees are in each section? ....(2 marks)

6 A school hall has 1596 chairs in it.
The chairs are placed in rows and there are 38 chairs in each row.

How many rows are there? ....(1 mark)

7 A shop buys 126 sweaters.
If each sweater is sold for £65, how much money does the shop take in total?

....(2 marks)

Score .... /14

S **These are SATs-style questions. Answer all parts of the questions.**

1   There are forty-five pencils in a box.
    A box of pencils costs £3·50.

    a) How many pencils are there in 6 boxes?   .... pencils   **(1 mark)**

    b) How much do 7 boxes cost?   £ ....   **(1 mark)**

    c) How much do 135 pencils cost?   £ ....   **(1 mark)**

    d) How many boxes of pencils can be bought with £42?   .... boxes   **(1 mark)**

2   Fill in the missing numbers so
    that the answer is always 60.

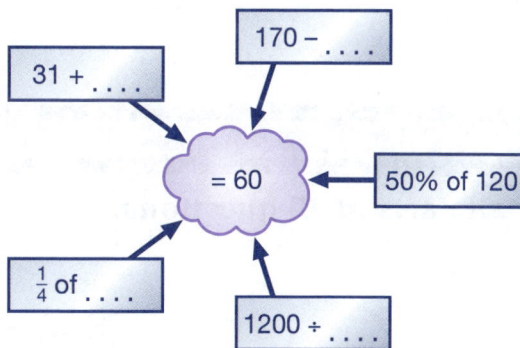

    $170 - \ldots$

    $31 + \ldots$

    $= 60$

    $50\% \text{ of } 120$

    $\frac{1}{4} \text{ of } \ldots$

    $1200 \div \ldots$

                                                                                  (4 marks)

3   Nigel owns a garden centre. He sells small shrubs for £6·75 each.

    a) Nigel sells 37 small shrubs one weekend to Mrs Robinson.
       How much does he get for the 37 shrubs?   £ ....   **(2 marks)**

    b) Each small shrub needs 60 grams of compost when it is planted.
       Mrs Robinson buys a sack of compost weighing 2000 grams.

       i) How many shrubs can be planted?   .... shrubs   **(2 marks)**

       ii) How much more compost does she need in order to plant all 37 shrubs?

                                                        .... grams   **(1 mark)**

4   Raj puts a three-digit whole number into his calculator.
    He multiplies it by 10.

    a) Fill in one other digit which you know must be on the calculator display.

       ☐ ☐ 4 ☐ ☐

                                                                                  (1 mark)

    b) Raj starts again with the same three-digit number. This time he multiplies it by 1000.
       Fill in all the digits that might be on the calculator display.

       ☐ 2 7 ☐ ☐ ☐

                                                                                  (1 mark)

    Score .... /15

TOTAL SCORE   /29

For more help on this topic see KS3 Maths Success Guide pages 8–9

FRACTIONS

M **Choose just one answer, a, b, c or d.**

1 In a class of 32 students, $\frac{3}{4}$ are right handed. How many students are right handed?

a) 8 b) 16 c) 26 d) 24 (1 mark)

2 Work out the answer to $\frac{5}{7} - \frac{1}{21}$.

a) $\frac{4}{14}$ b) $\frac{14}{21}$ c) $\frac{2}{7}$ d) $\frac{1}{3}$ (1 mark)

3 Work out the answer to $\frac{3}{5} \div \frac{4}{10}$.

a) $\frac{12}{60}$ b) $\frac{3}{2}$ c) $\frac{7}{15}$ d) $\frac{12}{15}$ (1 mark)

4 Work out the answer to $\frac{2}{9} \times \frac{3}{11}$.

a) $\frac{22}{27}$ b) $\frac{6}{9}$ c) $\frac{5}{20}$ d) $\frac{6}{99}$ (1 mark)

Score .... /4

Q **Answer all parts of all questions.**

1 Work out the following:

a) $\frac{2}{7} + \frac{3}{5} =$ ....

b) $\frac{8}{13} - \frac{1}{2} =$ .... (2 marks)

2 Arrange these fractions in order of size, smallest first.

a) $\frac{4}{5}, \frac{1}{3}, \frac{2}{9}, \frac{4}{7}, \frac{1}{2}$ ....

b) $\frac{9}{13}, \frac{3}{5}, \frac{2}{7}, \frac{1}{3}$ .... (2 marks)

3 Work out the following:

a) $\frac{2}{7} \times \frac{4}{9}$ ....

b) $\frac{6}{7} \div \frac{3}{14}$ ....

c) $\frac{9}{11} \times \frac{2}{5}$ ....

d) $\frac{4}{5} \div \frac{3}{10}$ .... (4 marks)

4 Work out the answer to each statement and decide whether it is true or false.

a) $\frac{3}{5}$ of 20 is greater than $\frac{2}{7}$ of 14. .... (1 mark)

b) $\frac{9}{11}$ of 44 is smaller than $\frac{1}{3}$ of 72. .... (1 mark)

c) $\frac{2}{7}$ of 21 is greater than $\frac{3}{5}$ of 15. .... (1 mark)

d) $\frac{1}{3}$ of 27 is smaller than $\frac{5}{9}$ of 45. .... (1 mark)

5 The village of Grimley has 2200 inhabitants. $\frac{3}{5}$ of the inhabitants are men. How many men are in the village? .... (1 mark)

6 Mark has a fruit stall. $\frac{2}{7}$ of the fruit he has are apples. If he has 245 pieces of fruit in total, how many are apples? .... (1 mark)

7 A hospital has 350 pints of milk delivered. If $\frac{2}{5}$ of the milk is skimmed, how many pints are not skimmed? .... (1 mark)

Score .... /15

These are SATs-style questions. Answer all parts of the questions.

1   Rani and David bake some cakes. They have 16 cakes each.

    a) Rani eats a quarter of her cakes.
       How many cakes does Rani eat?...(1 mark)

    b) David eats 12 of his 16 cakes.
       What fraction of his cakes does David eat? .... (1 mark)

    c) How many cakes are left altogether? .... (1 mark)

2   Fill in the missing values so that the answer is always 8.

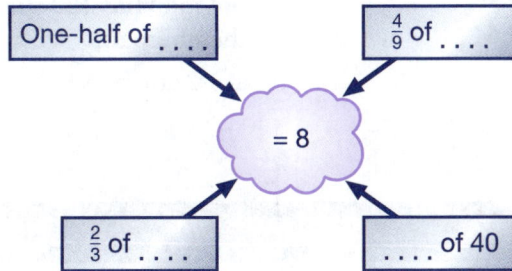

One-half of		$\frac{4}{9}$ of . . . .
	= 8	
$\frac{2}{3}$ of		. . . . of 40

                                                                          (4 marks)

3   Carry out these calculations.

    a) $\frac{1}{2}$ of £60   ....   (1 mark)

    b) $\frac{2}{3}$ of £900   ....   (1 mark)

    c) $\frac{2}{7} + \frac{3}{5}$ ....   (1 mark)

    d) $\frac{4}{7} \times \frac{2}{5}$ ....   (1 mark)

4   In a book there are three pictures on the same page.

    Picture 1 uses $\frac{1}{4}$ of the page.

    Picture 2 uses $\frac{1}{16}$ of the page.

    Picture 3 uses $\frac{1}{64}$ of the page.

    a) In total, what fraction of the page do pictures 1 and 2 make up?........................ (2 marks)

    b) To put a picture in a book is more expensive than text.

             Cost of picture = £35 for every $\frac{1}{8}$ of a page

    If a picture takes up $\frac{3}{32}$ of a page, how much will it cost? .... (1 mark)

                                                    Score .... /14

TOTAL SCORE   /33

For more help on this topic see KS3 Maths Success Guide pages 10–11

DECIMALS

M Choose just one answer, a, b, c or d.

1 Work out the answer to 9.23×6.

a) 55·83 b) 54·83 c) 54·38 d) 55·38   (1 mark)

2 Round 17·26 to one decimal place.

a) 17·3 b) 17·2 c) 1·726 d) 1·73   (1 mark)

3 Round 14·635 to two decimal places.

a) 14·63 b) 14·65 c) 146·35 d) 14·64   (1 mark)

4 If a piece of cake weighs 0·2 kg, how much would 60 identical pieces of cake weigh?

a) 0·12 kg b) 1·2 kg c) 12 kg d) 120 kg   (1 mark)

5 A piece of writing paper is 0·01 cm thick. A notepad has 120 sheets of paper. How thick is the notepad?

a) 1·2 cm b) 0·12 cm c) 12 cm d) 120 cm (1 mark)

Score .... /5

Q Answer all parts of all questions.

1 Here are some numbers:

4·39   3·69   3·691   2·71   4·385   3·62   4·38

Arrange these numbers in order of size, smallest first.

.... (2 marks)

2 The number pyramid below is found by adding the two numbers in the row below.

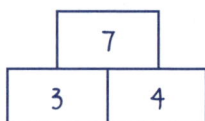

```
    7
  3   4
```

Complete this pyramid.

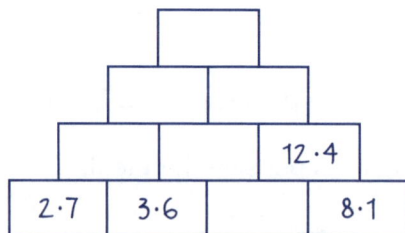

```

          12·4
 2·7  3·6      8·1
```

(4 marks)

3 Four friends are playing a game. Their scores are shown below:

Tom	Ahmed	Rebecca	Lin
4·27	4·98	5·07	5·065

a) Who won the game, with the highest score? .... (1 mark)

b) What is the difference between Ahmed's and Lin's scores? .... (1 mark)

4 A CD costs £11·58. James buys six. How much must he pay for the six CDs?

.... (1 mark)

5 For each statement decide whether it is true or false.

a) 2·73 rounded to 1 decimal place is 2·7...(1 mark)

b) 12·738 rounded to 2 decimal places is 2·73...(1 mark)

c) 25·621 rounded to 1 decimal place is 25·2..(1 mark)

6 Here are some number cards:

| 0·1 | 0·01 | 0·001 | 100 | 10 |

Fill in each gap using one of the number cards to make the statement correct.

a) 4 × .... = 0·04   b) 60 × .... = 0·06

c) 500 × .... = 5000   d) 30 × .... = 0·03

e) 5 ÷ .... = 50   f) 60 ÷ .... = 60000

g) 25 ÷ .... = 2500   h) 32 ÷ .... = 320   (8 marks)

Score .... /20

S These are SATs-style questions. Answer all parts of the questions.

1 Complete these calculations to make them correct.

a) 14·6 + 3·9 = 12·1 + ...   (1 mark)

b) 8·3 × 4 = 2 × ....   (1 mark)

c) 937·65 − 2·3 = 654·1 + ...   (1 mark)

d) 124·8 ÷ 4 = 2 × ....   (1 mark)

2 Look at these number cards:

| 0·3 | 3 | 10 | 1 | 0·02 | 0·5 | 0·01 |

a) Choose two of the cards to make the smallest possible answer.

[ ] × [ ] = ...   (3 marks)

b) Choose two of the cards to give the answer 150.

[ ] ÷ [ ] = 150   (2 marks)

c) Choose two of the cards to give the answer 1000.

[ ] ÷ [ ] = 1000   (2 marks)

Score .... /11

TOTAL SCORE   /36

For more help on this topic see KS3 Maths Success Guide pages 12–13

PERCENTAGES 1

Q | **Answer all parts of all questions.**

1 The building society has reported a 10% rise in house prices over the last year. If the average price of a house last year was £90 000, what is the average house price this year? ....(2 marks)

2 A shoe shop is having a sale:

> **Shoe World**
> **15% off**
> **marked prices**

A pair of trainers originally cost £130.

What is the sale price of the trainers? ....(2 marks)

3 Match the calculations with the correct answers. The first has been done for you.

10% of 60	32
25% of 200	45
40% of 80	6
15% of 120	18
30% of 150	50

(4 marks)

4 Police reported an increase in burglaries last year of 15%. If 620 burglaries had been committed the year before, how many more burglaries had been committed?

.... (1 mark)

5 A train ticket from Manchester to Birmingham costs £24 return. If you book in advance, the price of the ticket is reduced by 6%.
What is the advanced booking price of the ticket? .... (1 mark)

6 These are some of the results for Hywel's end of year examinations:

Maths   64 out of 80   = ...%   English   27 out of 50   = ...%

Geography 39 out of 42   = ...%   Science   121 out of 150   = ...%

German   42 out of 110   = ...%

a) Change each of the results into a percentage.   (2 marks)

b) In which subject did Hywel do worst? .... (1 mark)

7 A survey showed the favourite packet of crisps, chosen by 500 people were the following:

Salt 'n' vinegar 204   Cheese 196   Beef 100

a) What percentage of people preferred cheese flavoured crisps? .... (2 marks)

b) What percentage of people did not like beef flavoured crisps? .... (2 marks)

Score .... /17

S These are SATs-style questions. Answer all parts of the questions.

1 Complete the missing values.

10% of £80 = £...(1 mark)

5% of £80 = £..(1 mark)

$2\frac{1}{2}$% of £80 = £..(1 mark)

$17\frac{1}{2}$% of £80 = £..(1 mark)

2 A cake shop sells some different types of cakes.
The table shows how many they sold in one day.

Cake	Number of cakes sold	Takings (£)
Doughnut	146	32·12
Battenberg	45	8·10
Coconut slice	37	20·35
Almond slice	48	41·76
Chocolate brownie	74	70·30
Total	350	172·63

a) What percentage of the number of cakes sold were doughnuts?

Show your working. ....% (2 marks)

b) What percentage of the total takings was for doughnuts?

Show your working. ....% (2 marks)

c) What percentage of the number of cakes sold were Battenberg?

Show your working. ....% (2 marks)

3 Calculate:

a) i) 4% of £32·50 = £...(1 mark)

ii) $12\frac{1}{2}$% of £78 = £...(1 mark)

b) A television costs £199. In a sale, 28% is taken off the price.
Work out the sale price of the television set.

£ ....(2 marks)

Score .... /14

TOTAL SCORE /31

For more help on this topic see KS3 Maths Success Guide pages 14–15

M Choose just one answer, a, b, c or d.

1 A shop bought a camera for £50.
A customer later buys the camera for £65.
Find the percentage profit.
a) 20% b) 15% c) 30% d) 40% (1 mark)

2 VAT at 17·5% is added to a telephone bill of £80.
What is the total amount to be paid?
a) £90 b) £95 c) £85 d) £94 (1 mark)

3 A house is bought for £80 000.
Each year the price rises by 10%.
How much is the house worth after 2 years?
a) £96 000 b) £98 000 c) £96 500 d) £96 800
(1 mark)

4 A sweater is bought in a sale for £20 after a
15% reduction.
What was the original price of the sweater?
a) £25 b) £23·53 c) £23·55 d) £23 (1 mark)

5 The price of a meal after VAT at 17·5% has been
added is £100.
What was the price of the meal before VAT?
a) £82·50 b) £87·50 c) £85·20 d) £85·11 (1 mark)

Score .... /5

Q Answer all parts of all questions.

1 John bought a sports car for £18 500. Two years later he sells the sports car
for £14 000. Work out the percentage loss.
....(2 marks)

2 On April 1st a train journey increases in price by 5%. Six months later it increases in
price again by 2%. Work out the final price of a ticket which originally cost £40.
.... (2 marks)

3 A car is bought for £12 000. Each year it depreciates in value by 5%. Work out the
value of the car after 3 years.
....(2 marks)

4 After a 7% rise, Frances is earning £390·55 per week. What was she earning before?
....(2 marks)

5 The Patel family paid £4525 for a holiday to New Zealand, after a 10% surcharge was
added at the last minute. What did they originally think they would be paying?
....(2 marks)

6 An electricity bill is £85 after a 5% reduction is made. How much was it originally?
....(2 marks)

Score .... /12

These are SATs-style questions. Answer all parts of the questions.

1   The table shows some information about pupils in a school:

	Wear glasses	Do not wear glasses
Girls	6	120
Boys	14	110

There are 250 pupils in this sample.

a) What percentage of the pupils are girls?

   Show your working.. % (2 marks)

b) The following month 2 more of the boys and 3 more of the girls have to wear glasses.
   Work out the percentage increase of those pupils who now wear glasses.
   (There are still 250 pupils in the sample.)

   Show your working.. % (2 marks)

2   A furniture shop had a closing down sale. The sale started on Wednesday and finished on Sunday. For each day of the sale, the prices were reduced by 20% of the prices of the day before.

a) A sofa had a price of £850 on Tuesday and it was bought on Friday. How much was it bought for?

   Show your working. .... (3 marks)

b) A sofa is bought on Thursday for £650. What was the price on Wednesday?

   Show your working. ....(2 marks)

c) Another shop is reducing its prices by 15% each day. How many days would it take for its original prices to be reduced by more than 50%?

   Show your working. .... days   (2 marks)

3   a) Roy sells used cars. He bought a car for £3570.
      Two days later he sold it for £5250. Work out his percentage profit.

   Show your working... % (2 marks)

   b) Roy sells a car for £6800. He makes a 30% profit.
      For what price did Roy buy the car? £...(2 marks)

Score .... /15

TOTAL SCORE   /32

FRACTIONS, DECIMALS, PERCENTAGES AND USING A CALCULATOR

Q **Answer all parts of all questions.**

1 Change these fractions into i) decimals and ii) percentages:

a) Fraction = $\frac{3}{5}$ i) decimal = ...   ii) percentage = ...% (2 marks)

b) Fraction = $\frac{1}{100}$ i) decimal = ...   ii) percentage = ...% (2 marks)

c) Fraction = $\frac{1}{8}$ i) decimal = ...   ii) percentage = ...% (2 marks)

2 Here are some cards. Divide the cards into four sets of three cards each showing the same value.

| 0·3 | $\frac{9}{20}$ | 0·1 | 45% | 25% | $\frac{3}{10}$ | 0·45 | $\frac{1}{4}$ | 30% | 10% | 0·25 | $\frac{1}{10}$ |

Set 1 ...., ..., ...   (1 mark)

Set 2 ...., ..., ...   (1 mark)

Set 3 ...., ..., ...   (1 mark)

Set 4 ...., ..., ...   (1 mark)

3 Here are some cards:

| $\frac{2}{5}$ | 72% | $\frac{3}{8}$ | 25% | 0·9 | 0·41 | 30% |

Put these cards in order of size, smallest first. ....(2 marks)

4 The same television is being sold in different shops.

SUPERS	ELECTRICALS	RAMONES
$\frac{1}{3}$ off	20% off	TV £375
TV £570	TV £510	plus VAT at 17·5%

Work out the price of the television in each of the three shops.

Which shop sells the television at the cheapest price? ....(4 marks)

5 Work out these calculations without using a calculator.

a) $5 + 3 \times 2 =$ ....

b) $(6 + 3) \times 4 =$ ....

c) $12 + 6 \div 2 =$ ....(3 marks)

6 Work out these calculations using a calculator:

a) $\dfrac{6·2 + 4·9}{3·7 \times 4·1}$

b) $\dfrac{\sqrt{10·3} - 2·1}{(2·3)^2}$

c) $\dfrac{9·3^2 \times 2}{\sqrt{5·6}}$

= ....   = ...   = ...   (3 marks)

Score ...... /22

20

These are SATs-style questions. Answer all parts of the questions.

1   Charlotte has some cards:

| 0·125 | 0·75 | $\frac{1}{2}$ | 0·4 | 40% | 50% |

Reece has some different cards:

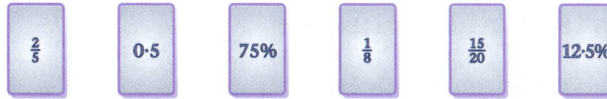

| $\frac{2}{5}$ | 0·5 | 75% | $\frac{1}{8}$ | $\frac{15}{20}$ | 12·5% |

They decide to group the cards together, so that in each group the cards are equivalent.
Complete the card groups below.

$\frac{2}{5}$, ..., ..., 0·5, ..., ..., 12·5%   ...., 0·75, ...   (4 marks)

2   A target board has some fractions, decimals and percentages:

0·55	$\frac{1}{25}$	$\frac{1}{3}$	$\frac{11}{20}$	$\frac{2}{7}$
$\frac{3}{8}$	20%	0·9	0·375	$\frac{1}{20}$
90%	$0·\dot{3}$	0.05	$\frac{2}{10}$	$\frac{9}{10}$
0·2	5%	37·5%	$33·\dot{3}\%$	55%

Here are some of the sets which are equivalent:

Set 1   55%,   0·55, $\frac{11}{20}$

Set 2   20%,   0·2, $\frac{2}{10}$

There are four other sets which are equivalent. Write them in the spaces provided.

Set 3   ...., ..., ...   (1 mark)

Set 4   ...., ..., ...   (1 mark)

Set 5   ...., ..., ...   (1 mark)

Set 6   ...., ..., ...   (1 mark)

3   Work out the values of the following. Give your answers to 1 decimal place.

a) $5·2 + 3 + \dfrac{4 \times \sqrt{3·1^2 + 4·3^2}}{4}$ .... (1 mark)

b) $\dfrac{1}{4} \times 5·2 \times 3·1 + \dfrac{(3·1^2 + 7·2^2)}{2}$ .... (1 mark)

c) $\dfrac{2}{5} \times \dfrac{\sqrt{3·1^2 - 1·1^2}}{4} + 12^2$ ....(1 mark)

Score .... /11

TOTAL SCORE   /33

For more help on this topic see KS3 Maths Success Guide pages 18–19

ESTIMATES AND CHECKING CALCULATIONS

Q **Answer all parts of all questions.**

1 Round each of these values to 3 significant figures.

a) 0·073156 ....

b) 276479 ....

c) 5215 ....

d) 0·370794 .... (4 marks)

2 25624 people attend a football match.

Write this number to 2 significant figures. ....(1 mark)

3 For each of these calculations round the numbers to 1 significant figure and work out an approximate answer.

a) 279 × 31 ....(1 mark)

b) 627 × 217 ....(1 mark)

c) 36·8 × 42·8 ....(1 mark)

d) 475 ÷ 22 ....(1 mark)

e) 630 ÷ 9·9 ....(1 mark)

4 Round each of the numbers to 1 significant figure and work out an approximate answer.

a) $\frac{19 + 41}{3 \cdot 1}$ ....(1 mark)

b) $\sqrt{3 \cdot 1 \times 20 \cdot 2}$ ....(1 mark)

c) $\left(\frac{27 \cdot 5}{2 \cdot 9}\right)^2$ ....(1 mark)

5 Write down suitable calculations you could use to check the answers to the following questions.

a) 2472 ÷ 6 = 412 ....(1 mark)

b) 932 × 5 = 4660 ....(1 mark)

c) 460 + 52 = 512 ....(1 mark)

d) 1054 − 307 = 747 ....(1 mark)

6 A train goes 502 km in 1·3 hours.
By rounding to 1 significant figure, give a rough estimate of its speed in kilometres per hour.

....(1 mark)

7 Paint is sold in 8-litre tins.
Gill needs 42 litres of paint. How many tins must she buy?

....(1 mark)

Score .... /19

These are SATs-style questions. Answer all parts of the questions.

1 The table below shows some numbers. Round the numbers to the given number of significant figures.

Number	3 significant figures	2 significant figures	1 significant figure
2·7364			
4275			
0·03865			

(9 marks)

2 An athletics club is taking part in the Commonwealth Games in Manchester. 715 athletes are competing in the Games.
They are going to travel by coaches.
Each coach can carry 49 people.

a) How many coaches do they need for the journey?

Show your working. .... (1 mark)

b) Each coach costs £365 to hire.

What is the total cost of the coaches?   £...(1 mark)

c) How much does each person pay to share the cost of the coach?

£..(1 mark)

3 a) Circle the best estimate for the answer to 62·57 ÷ 11·94.

    3   4   5   6   7   8   (1 mark)

b) Circle the best estimate for the answer to 49·3 × 19·9.

    900   1000   1100   1200   1300   (1 mark)

c) Estimate the answer to $\frac{41 \cdot 4 \times 20 \cdot 6}{3 \cdot 1 + 4 \cdot 85}$.

Give your answer to 1 significant figure..(1 mark)

d) Estimate the answer to $\frac{(807 \div 40 \cdot 13)^2}{4 \cdot 01 + 6 \cdot 1}$.

Give your answer to 1 significant figure..(1 mark)

Score .... /16

TOTAL SCORE   /35

For more help on this topic see KS3 Maths Success Guide pages 20–21

RATIO

Q **Answer all parts of all questions.**

1 For each of the following statements, write down if they are true or false.

a) The ratio 20 : 10 is the same as the ratio 2 : 1...(1 mark)

b) The ratio 25 : 35 is the same as the ratio 4 : 5. ....(1 mark)

c) The ratio 21 : 27 is the same as the ratio 7 : 9...(1 mark)

2 Write down each of the following ratios in the form 1 : n.

a) 20 : 30 ....   b) 3 : 5 ....   c) 6 : 2 ....   (3 marks)

3 Divide each amount in the given ratio.

a) £20 in the ratio 2 : 3...(1 mark)

b) £600 in the ratio 5 : 7..(1 mark)

4 In a wood there are 300 trees. The ratio of oak to ash trees is 2 : 13.
How many ash trees are there in the wood?

....(1 mark)

5 A photograph of length 27 cm is to be enlarged in the ratio 3 : 7.
What is the length of the enlarged photograph? ....(1 mark)

6 A recipe needs the following ingredients for 4 people.

Complete the recipe for 6 people.

4 people
150 g flour
2 eggs
200 g sugar

6 people
.................g flour
.................eggs
.................g sugar

(2 marks)

7 Seven bottles of coke cost £10·15. Work out the cost of twelve bottles of coke.

....(2 marks)

8 Toothpaste is sold in three different sized tubes.

50 ml = £1·24   75 ml = £1·96   100 ml = £2·42

Which of the tubes of toothpaste gives the best value for money?
You must show full working out in order to justify your answer.

....(3 marks)

Score ...... /17

These are SATs-style questions. Answer all parts of the questions.

1 a) One morning, Ahmed carried out a survey of the cars in a car park. He saw 10 red, 20 blue, 35 black and 50 silver cars. Complete the line below to show the ratios:

10 : 20 : .... : ....

2 : .... : .... : ....
(2 marks)

b) On another morning he carried out the survey again. He surveyed the same number of cars. The ratio of the cars this time is:

1 : 5 : 12 : 5

Complete the table which shows the number of cars of each colour which are in the car park.

Colour	Number
Red	
Blue	
Black	
Silver	

(4 marks)

2 A tin holds 200 g of baked beans.
The label on the tin shows this information:

```
200 g tin

Nutritional Information
Energy          150 kcal
Protein         9·4 g
Carbohydrate    27·3 g
Fat             0·4 g
```

Beans

200 g

a) How many grams of carbohydrate would a 450 g tin of baked beans provide?

Show your working. ....(2 marks)

b) On a different brand of baked beans, different information is shown:

```
250 g tin

Nutritional Information
Energy          165 kcal
Protein         10·8 g
Carbohydrate    29·0 g
Fat             0·62 g
```

A girl eats the same amount of baked beans from both tins.
Which tin provides her with more protein?

Show your working. ....(2 marks)

Score .... /10

TOTAL SCORE /27

For more help on this topic see KS3 Maths Success Guide pages 22–23

RATIO

INDICES

M Choose just one answer, a, b, c or d.

1 In index form, what is the value of $5^3 \times 5^8$?
a) 5^{24} b) 5^5 c) 2^5 d) 5^{11} (1 mark)

2 In index form, what is the value of $(3^5)^2$?
a) 10^3 b) 3^{10} c) 3^7 d) 3^3 (1 mark)

3 What is the value of 4^0?
a) 1 b) 4 c) 0 d) 16 (1 mark)

4 What is the value of 3^{-2}?
a) $\frac{1}{9}$ b) -9 c) 9 d) -6 (1 mark)

5 What is the value of $7^{10} \div 7^{-2}$ written in index form?
a) 7^8 b) 7^{12} c) 7^{20} d) 7^{14} (1 mark)

Score .... /5

Q Answer all parts of all questions.

1 For each of the following, decide whether the expression is true or false.

a) $a \times a \times a = a^3$ ....

b) $6 \times 6 \times 6 \times 6 = 6^4$ ....

c) $y \times y^3 \times y^2 = y^7$ ....

d) $c^2 \times 3 \times c^4 \times 4 = 12c^6$ ....

e) $3 \times x \times x^2 \times 5 \times y^3 = 8x^3y^3$ .... (5 marks)

2 Here are some cards with some expressions. Match each of the cards to the correct expression.

$5n^2$	$3n$	$6n^4$	$9n^5$	$4n^{-2}$

a) $3n \times 2n^3$ = ...

b) $27n^9 \div 3n^4$ = ...

c) $12n^2 \div 4n$ = ...

d) $5 \times n^2$ = ...

e) $16n^4 \div 4n^6$ = ... (5 marks)

3 Simplify the following expressions.

a) $2x \times 3x$ = ...

b) $9x^2 \times 4x^3$ = ...

c) $7m^3 \times 3m^4$ = ...

d) $12x^4 \div 3x$ = ...

e) $16x^9 \div 4x^7$ = ...

f) $16x \div 4x^3$ = ...

g) $\frac{12a^2b}{4a}$ = ...

h) $\frac{25a^3b^2}{5ab}$ = ... (8 marks)

4 Write these fractions using negative indices.

a) $\frac{1}{10^3}$

b) $\frac{2}{x^3}$

c) $\frac{3}{a^5}$

d) $\frac{1}{2}$ (4 marks)

Score .... /22

S **These are SATs-style questions. Answer all parts of the questions.**

1 Look at the table:

4^0	=	1
4^1	=	4
4^2	=	16
4^3	=	64
4^4	=	256
4^5	=	1 024
4^6	=	4 096
4^7	=	16 384
4^8	=	65 536

a) Explain how the table shows that $64 \times 256 = 16\,384$. ....(1 mark)

b) Use the table to help you work out the value of $\frac{16\,384}{16}$. ....(1 mark)

c) Use the table to help you work out the value of $\frac{65\,536}{64}$. ....(1 mark)

d) The units digit of 4^5 is 4. What is the units digit of 4^{10}? ....(1 mark)

2 Some expressions are written on cards:

$4a^3$ $17a^5b^{10}$ $3a^2$ $10a^5$ $\frac{3}{a^2}$ $12a^6$

$64a^6$ $10a^6$ $30a^5b^{10}$ $4a^4$ $30a^6b^{24}$

Choose the correct card to go with each of the expressions below when fully simplified.

a) $5a^2 \times 2a^3$ .... b) $12a^4 \div 3a$ ....

c) $9a^3 \div 3a^5$ .... d) $(4a^2)^3$ ....

e) $15a^2b^4 \times 2a^3b^6$ .... (5 marks)

3 a) Simplify the expression $\frac{a^4b^3}{a^2b^2}$ ....(1 mark)

b) Simplify the expression $\frac{a^5b^2 \times a^3b^2}{a^2b^2}$. ....(1 mark)

c) Show that $\frac{(a+b)}{(a-b)(a+b)^2} + \frac{(a-b)}{(a-b)^2(a+b)}$

simplifies to $\frac{2}{(a+b)(a-b)}$. ....(2 marks)

Score .... /13

TOTAL SCORE /40

For more help on this topic see KS3 Maths Success Guide pages 24–25

STANDARD INDEX FORM

Q **Answer all parts of all questions.**

1 Write these numbers in standard form:

a) 2 670 000 = ...

b) 0·03296 = ...

c) 0·0000595 = ...

d) 2 million = ... (4 marks)

2 Write as ordinary numbers:

a) $2·5 \times 10^4$ = ...

b) $6·02 \times 10^{-3}$ = ...

c) $9·03 \times 10^6$ = ...

d) $1·27 \times 10^{-5}$ = ... (4 marks)

3 For each of the questions below, decide whether the statements are true or false.

a) 2700 written in standard form is $2·7 \times 10^3$. ....

b) 0·036 written in standard form is $3·6 \times 10^2$. ....

c) 0·00027 written in standard form is 27×10^{-5}. ....

d) 251 000 written in standard form is $2·51 \times 10^5$. ....(4 marks)

4 Carry out the following calculations, giving your answers in standard form.

a) $(3 \times 10^6) \times (2 \times 10^4)$ = ...

b) $(5 \times 10^7) \times (3 \times 10^2)$ = ...

c) $(9 \times 10^5) \div (3 \times 10^2)$ = ...

d) $(1·6 \times 10^9) \div (4 \times 10^{-2})$ = ...(4 marks)

5 Work these out, giving your answers in standard form.

a) $(4·2 \times 10^8) \times (6·1 \times 10^5)$ = ...

b) $(9·3 \times 10^5) \times (3·6 \times 10^4)$ = ...

c) $(3·6 \times 10^{-4}) \times (3·8 \times 10^{-9})$ = ...

d) $(8·1 \times 10^{-2}) \times (4·2 \times 10^{-3})$ = ...

e) $(6·4 \times 10^9) \div (3·1 \times 10^4)$ = ...

f) $(6·9 \times 10^5) \div (2 \times 10^{-6})$ = ...(6 marks)

6 The mass of a hair is 0·000042 grams.

a) Write this number in standard form...............................(1 mark)

b) Calculate, in standard form, the mass of 6×10^5 hairs...............................(1 mark)

Score .... /24

S — These are SATs-style questions. Answer all parts of the questions.

1 Charlotte is carrying out a science project. She has found out the diameters of two planets in centimetres.

Planet A 1.3×10^9 cm

Planet B 3.5×10^8 cm

a) How many times bigger is the diameter of planet A than the diameter of planet B?

Show your working...(1 mark)

b) What is the difference in diameter between planet A and planet B?

....(1 mark)

c) The formula $4\pi r^2$, where r is the radius of the planet, is used to work out the surface area.

i) Work out the radius of planet A..cm   (1 mark)

ii) Work out the surface area of planet A, giving your answer in standard form.

Show your working. ....cm²   (2 marks)

2 $(3 \times 10^3) \times (2 \times 10^4)$ can be written simply as 6×10^7.
Write these values as simply as possible:

a) $(5 \times 10^3) \times (1 \times 10^6) = $ ....(1 mark)

b) $\dfrac{8 \times 10^9}{4 \times 10^{-2}} = $ ....(1 mark)

3 The mass of an atom is 2×10^{-23} grams.

What is the total mass of 9×10^{15} of these atoms?

Show your working. ....grams   (2 marks)

4 A building is sold for £6.2 million.

a) Write down 6.2 million in standard form. ....(1 mark)

b) Seven investors buy the building. How much does each investor pay?
Give your answer to 1 significant figure and write it in standard form.

....(2 marks)

Score .... /12

Q **Answer all parts of all questions.**

1 Write the following in symbols.

   a) 4 more than t .... b) 6 less than a ....

   c) 5 times a .... d) a divided by c ....

   e) 5 less than 4 times b .... f) 6 more than a, divided by n ....

   g) 4 less than half of y .... h) c less than a quarter of p ....

   (8 marks)

2 Simplify the following expressions.

   a) $a \times a \times a$ .... b) $2 \times a \times 3 \times b$ ....

   c) $a \times 3 \times a \times 4$ .... d) $6 \times b^2 \times c \times b \times 2$ .... (4 marks)

3 Here are some cards with expressions.

   Match each expression with the equivalent statement.

$m + 2$	five less than m		$2m$	two divided by m
$m - 5$	double m		$5 - m$	two more than m
$\dfrac{2}{m}$	m squared		$m \times m$	m less than 5

   (6 marks)

4 Decide whether these expressions which have been simplified are true or false.

   a) $5a + 2a = 7a$ .... b) $6a + 2b - b = 6a - b$ ....

   c) $3a - 5b + 2b = 3a + 3b$ .... d) $2a + 3a - 5a + 6b - b = 5b$ ....

   (4 marks)

5 For an algebra pyramid, the next layer is formed by adding the two boxes in the row below.
   Complete this algebra pyramid.
   Write each expression as simply as possible.

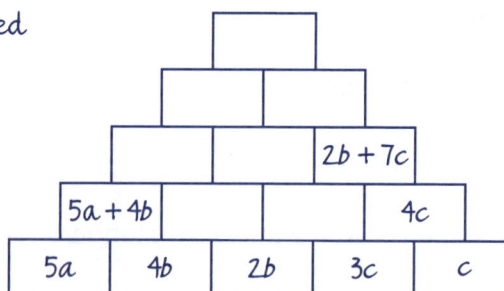

   (3 marks)

6 The diagram shows some patterns made up with mauve and white tiles.

   pattern 1   pattern 2   pattern 3

   Using p for the pattern number and t for the total number of tiles, complete this formula connecting p and t:

   $t =$ .... $\times p +$ ....

   (2 marks)

   Score .... /27

These are SATs-style questions. Answer all parts of the questions.

1 The perimeter of this shape is $2a + 2b$.

$p = 2a + 2b$

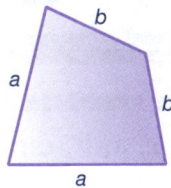

Write an expression for the perimeter of each of these shapes.
Write each expression in its simplest form.

a)

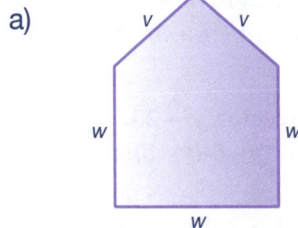

$p = $ .... (1 mark)

b)

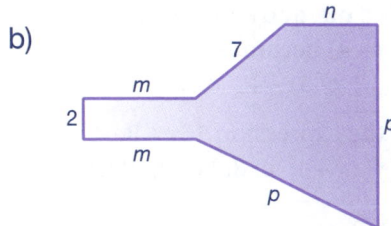

$p = $ .... (1 mark)

2 These patterns are made with matchsticks:

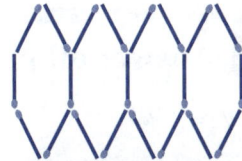

pattern 1 needs
6 matches

pattern 2 needs
11 matches

pattern 3 needs
16 matches

pattern 4 needs
21 matches

A rule to find how many matches are needed for each pattern is: $m = 5p + 1$
m stands for the number of matches.
p stands for the pattern number.

a) Use the rule to find the number of matches that would be needed in pattern number 10.

Show your working. ....(2 marks)

b) If 151 matches are used for another pattern, what would its pattern number be?

Show your working. ....(2 marks)

A different pattern is then made with the matches.

pattern 1 needs
5 matches

pattern 2 needs
9 matches

pattern 3 needs
13 matches

If p stands for the pattern number and m stands for the number of matches, write down a rule that connects p and m.

....(2 marks)

Score .... /8

TOTAL SCORE   /35

For more help on this topic see KS3 Maths Success Guide pages 30–31

ALGEBRA 2

M Choose just one answer, a, b, c or d.

1 If $v = mr$ and $m = 10$ and $r = 6$, what is the value of v?
a) 106 b) 610 c) 60 d) 16   (1 mark)

2 When multiplied out and simplified, the expression $3(5x - 4)$ becomes:
a) $15x$ b) $15x - 12$ c) $5x - 12$ d) $15x - 4$ (1 mark)

3 Factorise fully the expression $16x + 8$.
a) $2(8x + 4)$ b) $8(2x + 1)$ c) $8(2x)$ d) $4(4x + 2)$
                                                (1 mark)

4 Multiplied out and fully simplified, $(y - 2)^2$ is:
a) $y^2 - 2$ b) $y^2 + 4$ c) $y^2 - 4y + 4$ d) $y^2 + 4y + 4$
                                                (1 mark)

5 Factorise the expression $n^2 + 4n + 3$.
a) $(n - 1)(n - 3)$ b) $n(n + 4 + 3)$ c) $(n - 2)(n + 1)$
d) $(n + 1)(n + 3)$ (1 mark)

6 Factorise the expression $y^2 - 25$.
a) $(y + 5)(y - 10)$ b) $(y - 5)(y - 5)$ c) $(y - 5)(y + 5)$
d) $(y - 5)(y - 10)$ (1 mark)

Score .... /6

Q Answer all parts of all questions.

1 If $V = IR$:

a) Calculate V when $I = 24$ and $R = 2 \cdot 5$ .... (1 mark)

b) Calculate V when $I = 2 \cdot 7$ and $R = 10$ ....(1 mark)

c) Calculate R when $V = 65$ and $I = 5 \cdot 2$ ....(1 mark)

2 Expand and simplify the following expressions.

a) $2x(x + 1)$ ....(1 mark)

b) $(n + 2)(n + 3)$...(1 mark)

c) $(n - 3)(n - 4)$...(1 mark)

d) $(n - 3)^2$ ....(1 mark)

3 Factorise the following expressions.

a) $10n + 20$ ....   b) $12 - 24n$ ....

c) $15n + 30$ ....   (3 marks)

4 Rearrange each of the formulae below to make n the subject.

a) $a = bn$...(1 mark)

b) $r = 2n - 4$...(1 mark)

c) $a = \frac{3n}{2} + 1$...(1 mark)

d) $y = 2(n + 1)$...(1 mark)

5 Factorise the following expressions.

a) $n^2 + 6n + 5$...............................   b) $n^2 - 7n + 10$ ....

c) $n^2 - 64$ ....   (3 marks)

Score .... /17

These are SATs-style questions. Answer all parts of the questions.

1 a) Nilam uses this formula to calculate the perimeter (P) of a shape.

$$P = a + 2b + \frac{\sqrt{a^2 + b^2}}{4}$$

Work out the perimeter of the shape if $a = 3$ and $b = 4{\cdot}2$.

Show your working. ....(2 marks)

b) Naeve has a different shape. The formula to calculate the area (A) of the shape is given by:

$$A = r^2 + s^2 + \frac{4rs}{5}$$

Calculate the area of Naeve's shape when $r = 6$ and $s = 2{\cdot}6$.

Show your working. ....(2 marks)

2 a) Two of the expressions below are equivalent.
Circle them.

$3(y + 4)$　　　　　$2(4y + 3)$　　　　　$4(2y + 4)$

$3(y + 2)$　　　　　$2(4y + 8)$　　　　　$2(4y + 5)$　　　　　(1 mark)

b) Factorise this expression.

$6y + 12$ ....(1 mark)

c) Factorise fully this expression.

$4y^3 - 8y^2$ ....(2 marks)

d) Rearrange this formula to make y the subject.

$n = 4y - 3$ ....(1 mark)

e) Fully factorise the following expressions.

i) $p^2 + 3p - 10$ ....　ii) $p^2 - 6p + 9$ ....　(2 marks)

Score .... /11

TOTAL SCORE   /34

For more help on this topic see KS3 Maths Success Guide pages 32–33

EQUATIONS 1

M Choose just one answer, a, b, c or d.

1 Solve the equation $n - 3 = 7$.
a) 12 b) 2 c) 4 d) 10   (1 mark)

2 Solve the equation $3n - 1 = 11$.
a) 12 b) 36 c) 6 d) 4   (1 mark)

3 Solve the equation $5n + 4 = 19$.
a) 20 b) 3 c) 10 d) 5   (1 mark)

4 Solve the equation $3(x + 2) = 12$.
a) 8 b) 6 c) 2 d) 4   (1 mark)

5 Solve the equation $2(3 - 2y) = 3y - 8$.
a) 10 b) 5 c) 2 d) 6   (1 mark)

Score .... /5

Q Answer all parts of all questions.

1 Solve the following equations.

a) $2n = 12$ ....

b) $\frac{n}{3} = 4$ ....

c) $n + 3 = 10$ ....

d) $n - 9 = 12$ ....

e) $n - 3 = 4$ ....

f) $5n = 25$ ....

g) $\frac{n}{6} = 1$ ....

h) $2n - 1 = 9$ ....

i) $3n + 2 = 14$ ....

j) $\frac{n}{5} + 1 = 6$ ....

k) $5n + 3 = 18$ ....

l) $7n - 1 = 13$ ....

m) $\frac{n}{3} - 4 = 2$ ....   (13 marks)

2 Solve the following equations.

a) $5n + 1 = 3n + 7$ ....

b) $12n - 4 = 8n + 12$ ....

c) $10n + 3 = 7n + 5$ ....

d) $15n - 1 = 3n + 11$ ....   (4 marks)

3 Solve the following equations.

a) $5(3x - 1) = 20$ ....

b) $7(2x + 3) = 28$ ....

c) $4(n + 5) = 3(2n + 10)$ ....

d) $2(n - 5) = 4(n + 2)$ ....   (4 marks)

4 Solve the following equations.

a) $5n + 6 = 3(n + 1)$ ....

b) $2n - 3 + n = 2(n + 1)$ ....   (2 marks)

5 The angles in a triangle add up to 180°.
Form an equation in n and solve it for each of the shapes.   (6 marks)

a)
$n + 40°$
$n + 20°$
$2n$

b)
$3n + 30°$
$5n$
$2n + 40°$

c)
$n - 50°$
$4n + 10°$
$3n$

n = ...   n = ...   n = ...

Score .... /29

These are SATs-style questions. Answer all parts of the questions.

1   In this wall, each brick is made by adding the values of the bricks beneath it.

a) Fill in the missing expressions on this wall.

| .... |
| $3n + 2$ | .... |
| .... | n | $n + 2$ |

(3 marks)

b) If the value of the top brick is 24, work out the value of n.

$n =$ ....(1 mark)

2   This L shape is made with 8 square tiles:

This is a square tile. The edge of the tile is **a** centimetres long: a [ ] a

a) The perimeter of the L shape is 36 centimetres.
   Write an equation involving **a**.

....(1 mark)

b) Solve your equation to find the value of **a**.

a = ...(1 mark)

3   Solve these equations to find the values of v, w and x.

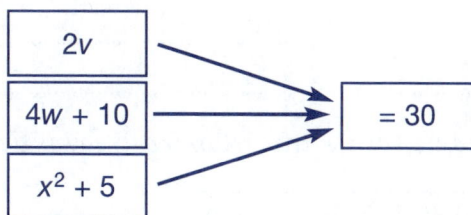

| $2v$ |
| $4w + 10$ | → | $= 30$ |
| $x^2 + 5$ |

$v =$ .... $w =$ .... $x =$ ....   (3 marks)

Score .... /9

TOTAL SCORE   /43

For more help on this topic see KS3 Maths Success Guide pages 34–35

EQUATIONS 2 AND INEQUALITIES

Q Answer all parts of all questions.

1 Solve the following simultaneous equations.

a) $x + y = 5$
   $2x - y = 4$ ....

b) $3x + 2y = 7$
   $5x - y = 3$ ....

c) $2x + y = 8$
   $3x - y = 2$ ....

d) $5x + 3y = 34$
   $4x - 3y = 11$ ....

e) $7x + 4y = 26$
   $3x + 3y = 15$ ....

f) $3x + 4y = 19$
   $4x - 3y = -8$ ....   (12 marks)

2

a) On the axes provided, draw the lines whose equations are:

   i) $x + y = 4$ Label this line P.   ii) $y = x - 2$ Label this line Q.   (2 marks)

b) Use the graphs to solve the simultaneous equations:

   $x + y = 4$, $y + x = 2$ x = ... y = ...   (2 marks)

3 Using a trial and improvement method, solve the following equations, giving your answer to 1 decimal place.

a) $a^2 - 104 = 0$ ....
   ....(1 mark)

b) $a^3 - a = 15$ ....
   ....(1 mark)

4 On the number lines provided, draw the following inequalities.

a) $x > -3$ $\overline{-5\ -4\ -3\ -2\ -1\ \ 0\ \ 1\ \ 2\ \ 3\ \ 4\ \ 5}$

b) $2 < x \le 5$ $\overline{-1\ \ 0\ \ 1\ \ 2\ \ 3\ \ 4\ \ 5\ \ 6\ \ 7\ \ 8\ \ 9}$ (2 marks)

5 Solve the following inequalities.

a) $5x + 2 < 12$ ....

b) $\frac{x}{3} + 1 \ge 3$ ....

c) $3 \le 2x + 1 \le 9$ ....

d) $3 \le 3x + 2 \le 8$ ....   (4 marks)

Score .... /24

These are SATs-style questions. Answer all parts of the questions.

1 Annabelle makes a rectangle with an area of 24·5 cm². The sides of Annabelle's rectangle are n cm and $(10 - n)$ cm.

$(10 - n)$

Area = 24·5 cm² n

She wants to find a value of n, to one decimal place, which gives her an area as close as possible to 24·5 cm². Use the table to find the value of n, to one decimal place.

n	$10 - n$	Area
2	8	16

n = ... (1 d.p.)

(3 marks)

2 Solve these simultaneous equations to find the values of a and b.

$4a + 3b$

$10a - 6b$

$= 36$

Show your working.

a = ... b = ...

(4 marks)

3 a) On the grid below, draw the graph $x + y = 4$.

   Shade in the region where $x + y \leq 4$.   (2 marks)

   b) On the same grid, draw the graph $y - x = 1$.

   Shade in the region where $y - x \geq 1$.   (2 marks)

   c) Label the region R where both these inequalities are satisfied.   (1 mark)

Score .... /12

TOTAL SCORE   /36

For more help on this topic see KS3 Maths Success Guide pages 36–39

NUMBER PATTERNS AND SEQUENCES

M Choose just one answer, a, b, c or d.

1 The rule for a sequence is: 'multiply the previous number by 2 and subtract 3'.
If the first term in the sequence is –2, what is the next term?
a) –1 b) 1 c) –7 d) 7 (1 mark)

2 What is the next number in this sequence?
3, 7, 11, 15
a) 20 b) 17 c) 18 d) 19 (1 mark)

3 What is the nth term of the sequence whose first four terms are 3, 7, 11, 15?
a) $n + 4$ b) $4n + 1$ c) $3n + 2$ d) $4n - 1$ (1 mark)

4 Here are the first four terms of a sequence:
2, 5, 10, 17
What is the nth term of this sequence?
a) $n + 3$ b) $n^2 + 1$ c) n^2 d) $n + 5$ (1 mark)

5 If the nth term of a sequence is given by $5n - 2$, what is the third term of the sequence?
a) 13 b) 15 c) 3 d) 17 (1 mark)

Score .... /5

Q Answer all parts of all questions.

1 Grace has written a sequence of numbers: 4, 7, 10, 13

a) Write down the next three terms in Grace's sequence. ....(1 mark)

b) What is the 10th term of this sequence? ....(1 mark)

c) What is the nth term of Grace's sequence? ....(1 mark)

2 Look at this sequence: 5, 9, 13, 17

a) What is the 6th number in this sequence? ....(1 mark)

b) Describe how this sequence is formed. ....(1 mark)

c) Write down the nth term of this sequence. ....(1 mark)

3 Look at this sequence of numbers: 3, 8, 15, 24

a) What is the next number in the sequence? ....(1 mark)

b) Write down the nth term of this sequence. ....(1 mark)

c) What is the 12th term of this sequence? ....(1 mark)

4 For each of these sequences, decide whether the nth term given is correct.

a) 2, 4, 6, 8, 10   nth term: $n + 2$ ....(1 mark)

b) 1, 4, 7, 10, 13   nth term: $3n - 2$ ....(1 mark)

c) 1, 4, 9, 16, 25   nth term: n^2 ....(1 mark)

Score .... /12

S These are SATs-style questions. Answer all parts of the questions.

1 a) This is a number sequence: 5, 8, 11, 14, ...

Write down the nth term of this number sequence.

....(1 mark)

b) This is another number sequence: 1, 4, 9, 16, ...

Write down the nth term of this number sequence.

....(1 mark)

2 Numbered squares are piled up. The diagram shows the first 4 rows.

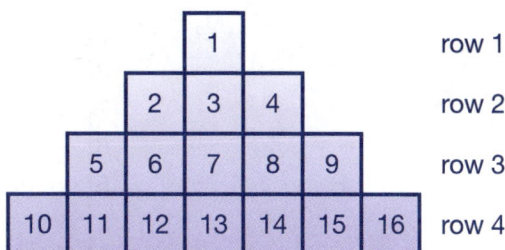

			1				row 1
		2	3	4			row 2
	5	6	7	8	9		row 3
10	11	12	13	14	15	16	row 4

a) The last number in row n is n^2.

For example, the last number in row 2 is $2^2 = 4$.

i) Calculate the last number in row 7. ....(1 mark)

ii) Calculate the first number in row 8. ....(1 mark)

b) The last number in row n is n^2.

Write an expression for the number that is two numbers before the last one in row n.

....(1 mark)

c) The first number in row n is $(n - 1)^2 + 1$.

Calculate the first number in the 10th row. ....(1 mark)

d) Write down an expression as simply as possible for the second number in row n.

....(1 mark)

e) Multiply out and simplify the expression $(n - 1)^2 + 1$. ....(1 mark)

Score .... /8

TOTAL SCORE   /25

For more help on this topic see KS3 Maths Success Guide pages 40–41

COORDINATES AND GRAPHS

Q Answer all parts of all questions.

1 a) Complete the table of values for each of these lines.

i) $y = 2x$

x	−2	−1	0	1	2	3
y						

ii) $y = 3x − 2$

x	−1	0	1	2	3
y					

(2 marks)

b) Draw the graphs

$y = 2x$ and $y = 3x − 2$
on the grid opposite.

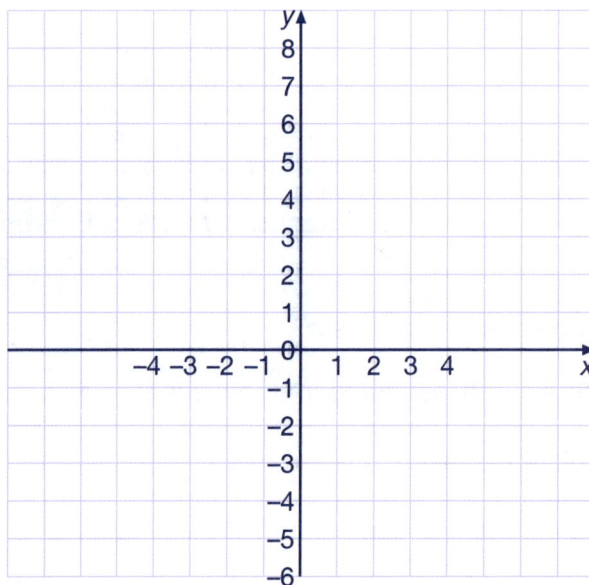

(2 marks)

2 The diagram below shows some straight-line graphs. Write down the equation of each line.

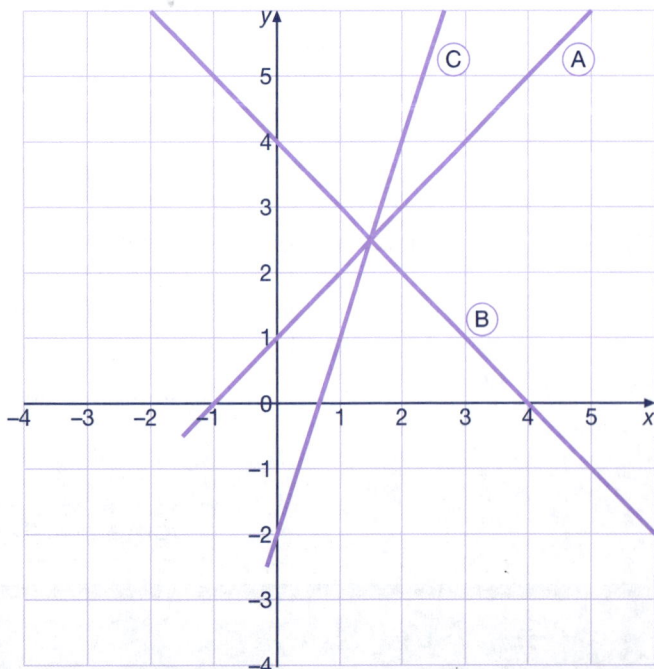

Line A: .... (1 mark)

Line B: .... (1 mark)

Line C: .... (1 mark)

Score .... /7

These are SATs-style questions. Answer all parts of the questions.

1 The diagram shows the graph of the line $y = 3x$.

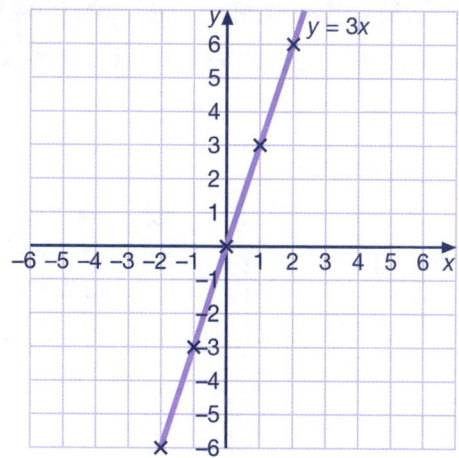

a) The straight line with the equation $y = 2x - 1$ goes through the point (3, 5).

i) Work out two more coordinates that lie on the line $y = 2x - 1$.

(..............., ...)   (..............., ...)   (2 marks)

ii) On the diagram above, draw the graph of the straight line $y = 2x - 1$.

Label your line $y = 2x - 1$.   (2 marks)

b) Write the equation of a straight line that goes through the point (0, –4) and is parallel to the straight line $y = 3x$.

$y =$ ....(1 mark)

2 Here are five different equations, labelled A to E.

| A | $y = 5x + 4$ |

| B | $y = 5 - 2x$ |

| C | $y = 4x + 1$ |

| D | $x + y = 5$ |

| E | $y = -3$ |

Think about the graphs of these equations.

a) Which graph goes through the point (0, 1)? ....(1 mark)

b) Which graph is parallel to the x-axis? ....(1 mark)

c) Which graph is parallel to $y = 5x - 2$? ....(1 mark)

d) Which two graphs meet at the point (0, 5)? ....(2 marks)

Score .... /10

TOTAL SCORE   /17

For more help on this topic see KS3 Maths Success Guide pages 42–43

MORE GRAPHS

Q **Answer all parts of all questions.**

1 Complete the tables for the graphs of:

a) i) $y = x^2$

x	-3	-2	-1	0	1	2	3
y			1			4	

ii) $y = 2x^2 - 4$

x	-3	-2	-1	0	1	2	3
y	14			-4		4	

b) Draw the graphs on the grid opposite.

(4 marks)

2 Match each of the sketch graphs to the equations below.

| $y = \frac{2}{x}$ | $y = x^2$ | $y = x^2 + 1$ | $y = x^3$ | $y = 2x^2 - 3$ | $y = x^2 - 6$ |

    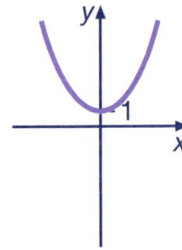

Equation:

a) .... b) .... c) .... d) .... e) ....

(5 marks)

3 For each of the functions below, state whether it is a linear or a quadratic function.

a) $y = x^2 - 4$ .... b) $y = 3 - 2x$ ....

c) $y = 6x - 1$ .... d) $y = 4x^2 - 2x + 1$ ....   (4 marks)

Score .... /13

These are SATs-style questions. Answer all parts of the questions.

1 The table below shows the value of x and y for the equation $y = x^2 - 4$.

a) Complete the table.

x	−2	−1	0	1	2	3
y				−3	0	5

(2 marks)

b) On the grid opposite, draw the graph.
Make sure you label the graph.

(2 marks)

c) On the same grid, sketch the graph of $y = x^2 + 2$. (1 mark)

d) Write down the equation of the line of symmetry of these graphs.

....(1 mark)

2 Here are seven different equations labelled A to G:

A	$y = x^2 - 4$

B	$y = x^2$

C	$y = 3x$

D	$y = 4 - x^2$

E	$x + y = 12$

F	$y = x^3$

G	$xy = 5$

Think about the graphs of these equations.

a) Which three graphs go through the point (0, 0)?

...., ... and ....   (3 marks)

b) Which graph goes through the point (3, 27)? ....(1 mark)

c) Which graphs are symmetrical about the y-axis?...(1 mark)

d) Which graph goes through the point (1, 3)?...(1 mark)

e) Which graph goes through the point (1, 5)?...(1 mark)

Score .... /13

TOTAL SCORE   /26

For more help on this topic see KS3 Maths Success Guide pages 44–45

INTERPRETING GRAPHS

Q **Answer all parts of all questions.**

1 This conversion graph converts British pounds (£) into euros (€) and vice versa.

Use the graph to convert:

a) £10 into euros .... (1 mark)

b) €16 into pounds.. (1 mark)

2 Amy has a mobile phone. Her mobile has this tariff:

Monthly charge £10.
Calls cost 10p per minute.

a) Complete the table which shows Amy's costs:

Number of minutes	0	10	20	30	40	50	60
Cost (£)	10			13			16

(2 marks)

b) Draw the graph showing Amy's costs on the axes provided.

(1 mark)

c) How much would 35 minutes of calls cost?

....(1 mark)

d) If Amy pays £25, for how many minutes did she use the phone that month?

....(1 mark)

e) Explain why Amy's bill cannot be less than £10.

....(1 mark)

Score .... /8

These are SATs-style questions. Answer all parts of the questions.

1

A   B   C   D

Here are four containers. Water is poured at a constant rate into three of the containers.
The graphs show the **depth** of the water as the containers fill up.

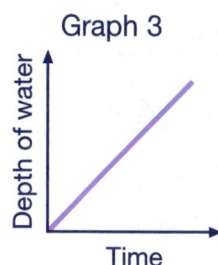

Graph 1

Graph 2

Graph 3

Fill in the gaps below to show which container matches each graph.

Graph 1 matches container ....   Graph 2 matches container ....

Graph 3 matches container ....   **(3 marks)**

2   The simplified graph shows the journey of a taxi travelling from London to St Albans.

a) What is the taxi's average speed from London to St Albans? .... mph **(1 mark)**

b) Explain what has happened at P.

    ....**(1 mark)**

c) A different taxi travels from St Albans to London. It sets off at 0720 and drives at a constant speed directly to London, arriving at 0745.

    On the graph, show the taxi's journey from St Albans to London.   **(2 marks)**

d) At approximately what time do the two taxis pass each other?

    ....**(1 mark)**

Score ...... /8

TOTAL SCORE   /16

For more help on this topic see KS3 Maths Success Guide pages 46–47

SHANES

Q **Answer all parts of all questions.**

1 The shapes below are triangles. Which of these words best describes each of them:

| Equilateral | Isosceles | Scalene |

a)   b)   c)

a is ....   b is ....   c is ....   (3 marks)

2 The lettered shapes are quadrilaterals. Decide whether each of the statements below is true or false.

a) Shape A is a parallelogram. ....   b) Shape B is a kite. ....

c) Shape C is a parallelogram. ....   d) Shape D is a rectangle. ....

e) Shape E is a square.   ....   (5 marks)

3 Complete the missing words in these statements.

a) A trapezium has one pair of .... sides.

b) A parallelogram has rotational symmetry of order ....

c) A square has .... lines of symmetry.

d) The perimeter of a circle is known as the ....

e) The radius and tangent to a point make an angle of ....   (5 marks)

4 Draw a regular hexagon.   (1 mark)

a) How many lines of symmetry does it have?..(1 mark)

b) What is its order of rotational symmetry?..(1 mark)

Score .... /16

S | **These are SATs-style questions. Answer all parts of the questions.**

1 a) Look at this shape. Two of the statements below are correct.
      Tick the correct statements.

      The shape is a hexagon. ☐

      The shape is a quadrilateral. ☐

      The shape is a kite. ☐

      The shape is a trapezium. ☐

      The shape is a parallelogram. ☐

(1 mark)

   b) Look at this shape. Complete these statements
      about the shape.

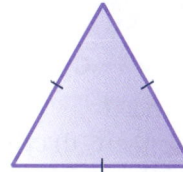

      The shape is an .... triangle. The shape has .... lines of symmetry.

      Each angle is .... degrees.

(3 marks)

2 Some names of polygons have been written on cards.

   Write down the name of the polygon for each of the shapes below, choosing from the list
   above.

   a)   b)   c)   d)

   a) ....   b) ....

   c) ....   d) ....   (4 marks)

3 In the space provided, draw an example of each of the shapes listed.

   a) Circle   b) Pentagon

   c) Parallelogram   d) Kite   (4 marks)

   a)   b)   c)   d)

Score .... /12

SOLIDS

M Choose just one answer, a, b, c or d.

Questions 1–5 relate to the diagrams drawn below.

A　　**B**　　**C**　　**D**

1 What is shape A known as?
a) cube b) cuboid c) sphere d) cylinder (1 mark)

2 What is the name given to shape B?
a) cube b) cylinder c) cone d) sphere (1 mark)

3 What is the name of shape C?
a) cylinder b) cone c) sphere d) rhombus
(1 mark)

4 How many faces does shape D have?
a) 4 b) 12 c) 8 d) 6 (1 mark)

5 If the plan of shape C is drawn, what shape would it be?
a) pentagon b) rectangle c) circle d) square
(1 mark)

Score .... /5

Q Answer all parts of all questions.

1 Which of the following nets would make a cube? ....(1 mark)

a)　　　　　b)　　　　　c)　　　　　d)　　　　　e)

a) How many edges does a cube have? ....(1 mark)

b) How many vertices does a cube have? ....(1 mark)

2 For this shape draw:
　a) a plan
　b) the elevation from B.

B

(2 marks)

Score .... /5

48

Letts

KS3

VISUAL
REVISION
GUIDE

SUCCESS

QUESTIONS & ANSWERS

MATHEMATICS
Levels 5-8

Fiona Mapp

ANSWER BOOK

Numbers (pages 6–7)
Box M
1 a
2 d
3 c
4 d
5 a
6 a

Box Q
1
a) 1, 4, 6, 12
b) 13, 17
c) 1, 4, 49
d) 6, 12
2   1   3   5   6   10   15
3   24
4   2
5   $2 \times 2 \times 3 \times 5$
6   False
7   1, 2, 3, 4, 6, 8, 12, 24
8
a) $4^3 = 4 \times 4 \times 4$
b) $2^5 = 2 \times 2 \times 2 \times 2 \times 2$

Box S
1
a) ○ ○ ○ ○ ○ ○
   ○ ○ ○ ○ ○ ○
b) ○ ○ ○ ○ ○ ○ ○ ○ ○ ○ ○ ○
c)

Number of rows	Number of counters in each row
1 row	12 counters in each row
2 rows	6 counters in each row
3 rows	4 counters in each row
4 rows	3 counters in each row
6 rows	2 counters in each row
12 rows	1 counter in each row

d) 5 is not a factor of 12
2   Penelope's number is 16
   Tom's number is 2

Positive and negative numbers (pages 8–9)
Box Q
1
a) –3 and –7
b) 0 and –7
c) 5 and –3
2
a) 12
b) 8
c) 12
d) –3
e) 3
f) –4
3
a) 21
b) –5
c) –2
d) –16
4   –22°C
5

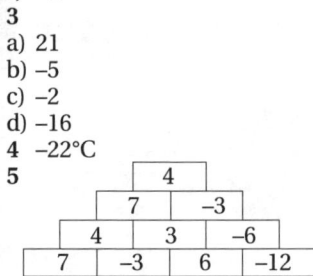

		4		
	7		–3	
4		3		–6
7	–3		6	–12

6
a) $-12 \div -3 = 4$
b) $-7 - (-3) = -4$
c) $9 \div -3 = -3$
d) $12 + (-5) = 7$

Box S
1
a) Arrow points to 32°C
b) Arrow points to –7°C
c) –2°C
d) 12°C
e) 15°C, 9°C, 0°C, –3°C, –6°C, –12°C
2
a) –1
b) –5
c) 5
d) –5
e) 3
f) –5

Working with numbers
Box Q (pages 10–11)
1
a) A and C
b) D
2

6	1	8
7	5	3
2	9	4

3
a) 11718
b) 529 620
c) 45
d) 83
4   £26·64
5   42
6   42
7   £8190

Box S
1
a) 270 pencils
b) £24·50
c) £10·50
d) 12 boxes
2
170 – 110
1200 ÷ 20
$\frac{1}{4}$ of 240
31 + 29
3
a) £249·75
b) (i) 33 shrubs
   (ii) 220 grams
4
a)

4		0

b)

4	2	7	0	0	0

Fractions (pages 12–13)
Box M
1 d
2 b
3 b
4 d

Box Q
1
a) $\frac{31}{35}$
b) $\frac{3}{26}$
2
a) $\frac{2}{9}, \frac{1}{3}, \frac{1}{2}, \frac{4}{7}, \frac{4}{5}$
b) $\frac{2}{7}, \frac{1}{3}, \frac{3}{5}, \frac{9}{13}$
3
a) $\frac{8}{63}$
b) 4
c) $\frac{18}{55}$
d) $2\frac{2}{3}$

4
a) True
b) False
c) False
d) True
5   1320
6   70
7   210

Box S
1
a) 4 cakes
b) $\frac{12}{16} = \frac{3}{4}$
c) 16 cakes
2
$\frac{4}{9}$ of 18
$\frac{1}{5}$ of 40
$\frac{2}{3}$ of 12
One-half of 16
3
a) £30
b) £600
c) $\frac{31}{35}$
d) $\frac{8}{35}$
4
a) $\frac{5}{16}$
b) £26·25

Decimals (pages 14–15)
Box M
1 d
2 a
3 d
4 c
5 a

Box Q
1   2·71, 3·62, 3·69, 3·691, 4·38, 4·385, 4·39
2

		34·5		
	14·2		20·3	
	6·3	7·9	12·4	
2·7	3·6	4·3	8·1	

3
a) Rebecca
b) 0·085
4   £69·48
5
a) True
b) False
c) False
6
a) 0·01   b) 0·001   c) 10
d) 0·001   e) 0·1   f) 0·001
g) 0·01   h) 0·1

Box S
1
a) 6·4
b) 16·6
c) 281·25
d) 15·6
2
a) $0·02 \times 0·01 = 0·0002$
b) $3 \div 0·02 = 150$
c) $10 \div 0·01 = 1000$

Percentages 1 (pages 16–17)
Box Q
1 £99 000
2 £110·50

3

10% of 60 → 32
25% of 200 → 45
40% of 80 → 6
15% of 120 → 18
30% of 150 → 50

4 93
5 £22·56
6
a) Maths   80%
   English   54%
   Geography   93%
   Science   81%
   German   38%
b) German
7
a) 39%
b) 80%

Box S
1
10% of £80 = £8
5% of £80 = £4
$2\frac{1}{2}$% of £80 = £2
$17\frac{1}{2}$% of £80 = £14
2
a) 41·7%
b) 18·6%
c) 12·9%
3
a) (i) £1·30
   (ii) £9·75
b) £143·28

Percentages 2 (pages 18–19)
Box M
1 c
2 d
3 d
4 b
5 d

Box Q
1 24%
2 £42·84
3 £10 288·50
4 £365
5 £4113·64
6 £89·47

Box S
1
a) 50·4%
b) 25% increase
2
a) £435·20
b) £812·50
c) 5 days
3
a) 47%
b) £5230·77

Fractions, decimals, percentages and using a calculator (pages 20–21)
Box Q
1
a) (i) 0·6   (ii) 60%
b) (i) 0·01   (ii) 1%
c) (i) 0·125   (ii) 12·5%
2
a) 0·3, $\frac{3}{10}$, 30%
b) 0·25, $\frac{1}{4}$, 25%
c) 0·1, $\frac{1}{10}$, 10%
d) 0·45, $\frac{9}{20}$, 45%

3 25%, 30%, $\frac{3}{8}$, $\frac{2}{5}$, 0·41, 72%, 0·9

4 Supers = £380
Electricals = £408
Ramones = £440·63
Supers is cheapest.

5
a) 11
b) 36
c) 15

6
a) 0·7317
b) 0·2097
c) 73·0974
(all to 4 d.p.)

Box S

1 $\frac{2}{5}$, 0·4, 40%
$\frac{1}{2}$, 0·5, 50%
$\frac{1}{8}$, 0·125, 12·5%
$\frac{15}{20}$, 0·75, 75%

2 90%, 0·9, $\frac{9}{10}$
33·$\dot{3}$%, 0·$\dot{3}$, $\frac{1}{3}$
37·5%, 0·375, $\frac{3}{8}$
5%, 0·05, $\frac{1}{20}$

3
a) 13·5 (1 d.p.)
b) 34·8 (1 d.p.)
c) 144·3 (1 d.p.)

Estimates and checking calculations (pages 22–23)
Box Q

1
a) 0·0732
b) 276 000
c) 5220
d) 0·371

2 26 000

3
a) 9000
b) 120 000
c) 1600
d) 25
e) 60

4
a) 20
b) 8
c) 100

5
a) 412 × 6 = 2472
b) 4660 ÷ 5 = 932
c) 512 − 52 = 460
d) 747 + 307 = 1054

6 500 km/h

7 6 tins of paint.

Box S

1

Number	3 s.f.	2 s.f.	1 s.f.
2·7364	2·74	2·7	3
4275	4280	4300	4000
0·03865	0·0387	0·039	0·04

2
a) 15 coaches
b) £5475
c) £7·66

3
a) 5
b) 1000
c) 100
d) 40

Ratio (pages 24–25)
Box Q

1
a) True
b) False
c) True

2
a) 1 : 1·5
b) 1 : 1·$\dot{6}$
c) 1 : 0·$\dot{3}$

3
a) 8 : 12
b) 250 : 350

4 260 ash trees

5 63 cm

6 225 g flour
3 eggs
300 g sugar

7 £17·40

8 The 100 ml tube

Box S

1
a) 10 : 20 : 35 : 50
    2 : 4 : 7 : 10

Colour	Number
Red	5
Blue	25
Black	60
Silver	25

2
a) 61·43 g (2 d.p.)
b) 200 g tin provides 0·047 grams of protein per gram of beans. 250 g tin provides 0·0432 g of protein per gram of beans, so the 200 g tin provides more protein.

Indices (pages 26–27)
Box M

1 d
2 b
3 a
4 a
5 b

Box Q

1
a) True
b) True
c) False
d) True
e) False

2
a) $6n^4$
b) $9n^5$
c) $3n$
d) $5n^2$
e) $4n^{-2}$

3
a) $6x^2$
b) $36x^5$
c) $21m^7$
d) $4x^3$
e) $4x^2$
f) $4x^{-2}$
g) $3ab$
h) $5a^2b$

4
a) 10^{-3}
b) $2x^{-3}$
c) $3a^{-5}$
d) 2^{-1}

Box S

1
a) 64 × 256
= $4^3 \times 4^4 = 4^7 = 16\,384$
b) $\frac{16\,384}{16} = \frac{4^7}{4^2} = 4^5 = 1024$
c) $\frac{65\,536}{64} = \frac{4^8}{4^3} = 4^5 = 1024$
d) $4^{10} = (4^5)^2$
    $4^2 = 16$
    units digit is 6

2
a) $10a^5$
b) $4a^3$
c) $\frac{3}{a^2}$
d) $64a^6$
e) $30a^5\,b^{10}$

3
a) a^2b
b) a^6b^2
c) $\frac{(a+b)}{(a-b)(a+b)^2} + \frac{(a-b)}{(a-b)^2(a+b)}$
$= \frac{1}{(a-b)(a+b)} + \frac{1}{(a-b)(a+b)}$
$= \frac{2}{(a+b)(a-b)}$

Standard index form (pages 28–29)
Box Q

1
a) $2·67 \times 10^6$
b) $3·296 \times 10^{-2}$
c) $5·95 \times 10^{-5}$
d) 2×10^6

2
a) 25 000
b) 0·00602
c) 9 030 000
d) 0·0000127

3
a) True
b) False
c) False
d) True

4
a) 6×10^{10}
b) $1·5 \times 10^{10}$
c) 3×10^3
d) 4×10^{10}

5
a) $2·562 \times 10^{14}$
b) $3·348 \times 10^{10}$
c) $1·368 \times 10^{-12}$
d) $3·402 \times 10^{-4}$
e) $2·06 \times 10^5$
f) $3·45 \times 10^{11}$

6
a) $4·2 \times 10^{-5}$
b) $2·52 \times 10^1$ grams

Box S

1
a) 3·7 times bigger
b) $9·5 \times 10^8$ cm
c) (i) $6·5 \times 10^8$ cm
    (ii) $5·3 \times 10^{18}$ cm^2

2
a) 5×10^9
b) 2×10^{11}

3 $1·8 \times 10^{-7}$ grams

4
a) $6\,200\,000 = 6·2 \times 10^6$
b) 9×10^5

Algebra 1 (pages 30–31)
Box Q

1
a) $t + 4$
b) $a − 6$

c) $5a$
d) $\frac{a}{c}$
e) $4b − 5$
f) $\frac{a+6}{n}$
g) $\frac{y}{2} − 4$
h) $\frac{p}{4} − c$

2
a) a^3
b) $6ab$
c) $12a^2$
d) $12b^3c$

3

$m + 2$	five less than m
$2m$	two divided by m
$m − 5$	double m
$5 − m$	two more than m
$\frac{2}{m}$	m squared
$m \times m$	m less than 5

4
a) True
b) False
c) False
d) True

5

$5a + 28b + 13c$			
$5a + 18b + 3c$	$10b + 10c$		
$5a + 10b$	$8b + 3c$	$2b + 7c$	
$5a + 4b$	$6b$	$2b + 3c$	$4c$
$5a$	$4b$	$2b$	$3c$	c

6
$t = 2 \times p + 3$

Box S

1
a) $p = 2v + 3w$
b) $p = 2p + 2m + n + 9$

2
a) $5 \times 10 + 1 = 51$ matches
b) pattern number 30
c) $m = 4p + 1$

Algebra 2 (pages 32–33)
Box M

1 c
2 b
3 b
4 c
5 d
6 c

Box Q

1
a) 60
b) 27
c) 12·5

2
a) $2x^2 + 2x$
b) $n^2 + 5n + 6$
c) $n^2 − 7n + 12$
d) $n^2 − 6n + 9$

3
a) $10(n + 2)$
b) $12(1 − 2n)$
c) $15(n + 2)$

4
a) $n = \frac{a}{b}$
b) $n = \frac{r+4}{2}$
c) $n = \frac{2(a-1)}{3}$
d) $n = \frac{y}{2} − 1$

5
a) $(n + 1)(n + 5)$
b) $(n − 2)(n − 5)$
c) $(n − 8)(n + 8)$

Box S

1

a) $P = 3 + (2 \times 4\cdot2) + \sqrt{\frac{(3^2 + 4\cdot2^2)}{4}}$
$P = 12\cdot69$

b) $A = 6^2 + 2\cdot6^2 + \frac{(4 \times 6 \times 2\cdot6)}{5}$
$A = 55\cdot24$

2

a) $4(2y + 4)$ and $2(4y + 8)$

b) $6(y + 2)$

c) $4y^2(y - 2)$

d) $y = \frac{n+3}{4}$

e) i) $(p - 2)(p + 5)$

   ii) $(p - 3)(p - 3)$

Equations 1 (pages 34–35)

Box M

1 d

2 d

3 b

4 c

5 c

Box Q

1

a) $n = 6$

b) $n = 12$

c) $n = 7$

d) $n = 21$

e) $n = 7$

f) $n = 5$

g) $n = 6$

h) $n = 5$

i) $n = 4$

j) $n = 25$

k) $n = 3$

l) $n = 2$

m) $n = 18$

2

a) $n = 3$

b) $n = 4$

c) $n = \frac{2}{3}$

d) $n = 1$

3

a) $x = \frac{5}{3}$

b) $x = \frac{1}{2}$

c) $n = -5$

d) $n = -9$

4

a) $n = -\frac{3}{2}$

b) $n = 5$

5

a) $n = 30°$

b) $n = 11°$

c) $n = 27\cdot5°$

Box S

1

a)

	5n + 4	
3n + 2	2n + 2	
2n + 2	n	n + 2

b) $n = 4$

2

a) $18a = 36$

b) $a = 2$

3

$v = 15$
$w = 5$
$x = \pm 5$

Equations 2 and inequalities (pages 36–37)

Box Q

1

a) $x = 3, y = 2$

b) $x = 1, y = 2$

c) $x = 2, y = 4$

d) $x = 5, y = 3$

e) $x = 2, y = 3$

f) $x = 1, y = 4$

2

a)

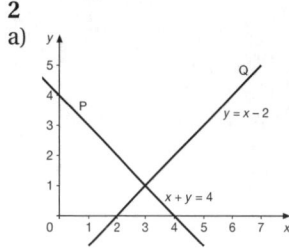

b) $x = 3, y = 1$

3

a) $a = 10\cdot2$

b) $a = 2\cdot6$

4 a)

b)

5

a) $x < 2$

b) $x \geq 6$

c) $1 \leq x \leq 4$

d) $\frac{1}{3} < x \leq 2$

Box S

1 $n = 4\cdot3$ cm

2 $a = 6, b = 4$

3

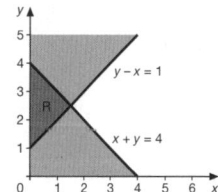

Number patterns and sequences (pages 38–39)

Box M

1 c

2 d

3 d

4 b

5 a

Box Q

1

a) 16, 19, 22

b) 31

c) $3n + 1$

2

a) 25

b) The gap between the numbers goes up by 4 each time.

c) $4n + 1$

3

a) 35

b) $n^2 + 2n$

c) 168

4

a) False

b) True

c) True

Box S

1

a) $3n + 2$

b) n^2

2

a) i) 49

   ii) 50

b) $n^2 - 2$

c) 82

d) $(n - 1)^2 + 2 = n^2 - 2n + 3$

e) $n^2 - 2n + 2$

Coordinates and graphs (pages 42–43)

Box Q

1

a) i) $y = 2x$

x	-2	-1	0	1	2	3
y	-4	-2	0	2	4	6

   ii) $y = 3x - 2$

x	-1	0	1	2	3
y	-5	-2	1	4	7

b)

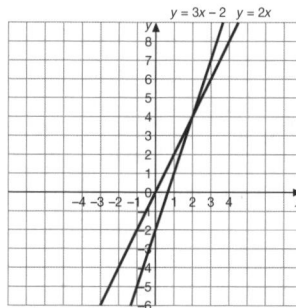

2

Line A: $y = x + 1$
Line B: $y = -x + 4$
Line C: $y = 3x - 2$

Box S

1

a) i) (2, 3) (0, -1)
(or any two points on the line)

   ii) See graph.

b) $y = 3x - 4$

2

a) C: $y = 4x + 1$

b) E: $y = -3$

c) A: $y = 5x + 4$

d) B: $y = 5 - 2x$
   D: $y + x = 5$

More graphs (pages 42–43)

Box Q

1

a) i) $y = x^2$

x	-3	-2	-1	0	1	2	3
y	9	4	1	0	1	4	9

   ii) $y = 2x^2 - 4$

x	-3	-2	-1	0	1	2	3
y	14	4	-2	-4	-2	4	14

b)

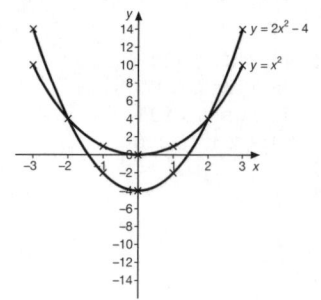

2

a) $y = x^2$

b) $y = 2x^2 - 3$

c) $y = \frac{2}{x}$

d) $y = x^3$

e) $y = x^2 + 1$

3

a) Quadratic function

b) Linear function

c) Linear function

d) Quadratic function

Box S

1

a)

x	-2	-1	0	1	2	3
y	0	-3	-4	-3	0	5

b) c)

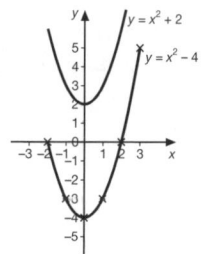

d) $x = 0$

2

a) $y = x^2, y = 3x, y = x^3$

b) $y = x^3$

c) $y = x^2 - 4, y = x^2, y = 4 - x^2$

d) $y = 4 - x^2$

e) $xy = 5$

Interpreting graphs (pages 44–45)

Box Q

1

a) approx. €16·50

b) £9·60

2

a)

Number of minutes	0	10	20	30	40	50	60
Cost (£)	10	11	12	13	14	15	16

b)

c) £13·50

d) 150 minutes

e) Even if Amy does not use her phone, she has to pay the £10 standing charge. So her bill will never be less than £10.

Box S

1
Graph 1 matches container D
Graph 2 matches container B
Graph 3 matches container A

2
a) 30 mph
b) Taxi has stopped.
c)

d) 0733

Shapes (pages 46–47)
Box Q

1
a is an isosceles triangle
b is a scalene triangle
c is an equilateral triangle

2
a) True
b) True
c) False
d) True
e) True

3
a) Parallel
b) 2
c) 4
d) Circumference
e) 90°

4

a) 6
b) 6

Box S

1
a) Trapezium and quadrilateral
b) Equilateral, 3, 60

2
a) Pentagon
b) Quadrilateral
c) Octagon
d) Heptagon

3

Solids (pages 48–49)
Box M

1 c
2 c
3 a
4 d
5 c

Box Q

1 Nets a, b, e
a) 12 edges
b) 8 vertices

2

a)   b)

Box S

1
a)

b)

2
a) Side view 2
   Side view 1
   Side view 4
   Side view 3
b)

Symmetry (pages 50–51)
Box M

1 c
2 c
3 d
4 b

Box Q

1

2
a) Order 1
b) Order 4
c) Order 4

3

a)   b)   c)

Box S

1

(Number of lines of symmetry)

		0	1	2	3	4
Order of	1		F			
rotational	2	E		A		
symmetry	3				B, D	
	4					C

2
a) All shapes should be identical on both sides.

---

b)

3
a) 2 planes of symmetry
b)

Constructions and LOGO (pages 52–53)
Box Q

1 Forward 6
  Turn right 120°
  Forward 6

2 Accurate diagrams to be drawn. Lengths accepted which are ± 2 mm.

3 Accurate diagrams to be drawn. Lengths to be accurate to ± 2 mm, angles to ± 2°.

4 Perpendicular bisector to be drawn at 3·5 cm.

5 Line bisects angle at 30°.

Box S

1
a) Forward 12
   Turn right 90°
   Forward 12
   Turn right 90°
   Forward 12
   Turn right 90°
   Forward 12
   Turn right 90°
   Forward 12
b) Forward 5
   Turn right 60°
   Forward 3
   Turn right 120°
   Forward 5
   Turn right 60°
   Forward 3

2 Accurate diagrams to be drawn. Lengths accepted which are ±2 mm.

Angles and tessellations (pages 54–55)
Box Q

1
a) 60°
b) 80°
c) 163°
d) 138°
e) 65°
f) 102°

2
a) $a = 130°$
   $b = 50°$
   $c = 50°$
b) $a = 60°$
   $b = 120°$
   $c = 60°$

3 20 sides

4 720°

5

Box S

1
a) i) $a = 80°$
   ii) $b = 20°$
b) $a = 65°$
   $b = 95°$
   $c = 150°$
c) i) $a = 60°$
      $b = 120°$
   ii) Three hexagons tessellate at a point, since $3 \times 120° = 360°$. Shapes will only tessellate when the angles add up to 360°.

Bearings and scale drawings (pages 56–57)
Box Q

1
a) (i) 072°   (ii) 252°
b) (i) 310°   (ii) 130°
c) (i) 230°   (ii) 050°
d) (i) 150°   (ii) 330°

2 Accurate diagrams to be drawn. Lengths to be accurate to ±2 mm, angles to ±2°.
Distance 9·8 km
Bearing 240°

3 10 km

Box S

1
a) Accurate diagrams to be drawn. Lengths to be accurate to ±2 mm, angles to ±2°.
b) 9·5 cm

2

not drawn to scale

Accurate diagrams to be drawn. Lengths to be accurate to ±2 mm, angles to ±2°.

b) 130 km

Transformations (pages 58–59)
Box M

1 b
2 c
3 d

Box Q

1

2
a) Reflection
b) Translation
c) Rotation
d) Reflection

Box S

1

mirror line | mirror line /

2

3

a)

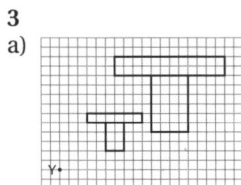

b) 12·5 cm and 3·6 cm

Loci and coordinates in 3D (pages 60–61)

Box Q

1
a) True
b) True
c) False
d) True

2

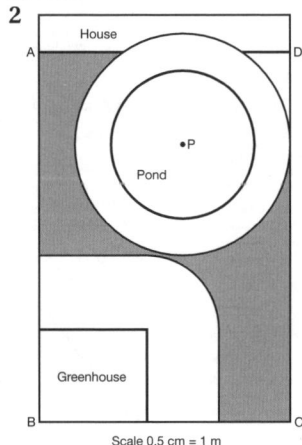

House

A   D

•P

Pond

Greenhouse

B   C

Scale 0.5 cm = 1 m

Box S

1

2

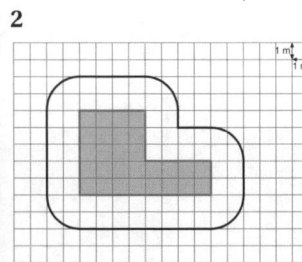

3 R = (3, 0, 3)
 S = (3, 3, 1)
 T = (0, 3, 1)

Pythagoras' Theorem (pages 62-63)

Box Q

1
a) Card D
b) Card F
c) Card A
d) Card E
e) Card B
f) Card C

2
$3^2 + 4^2 = 5^2$
$9 + 16 = 25$
Since Pythagoras' theorem works, it must be right angled.

3
a) RS = 7·8
b) VW = 3·6
c) XY = 4·5

4
24·1 cm

5
13·7 cm

Box S

1
540·8 km

2
$17^2 = 15^2 + 8^2$
$289 = 225 + 64$
Since Pythagoras' theorem works it must be right angled.

3
15·1 cm

4
a) RP is 5 cm because using Pythagoras' theorem:
 $4^2 + 3^2 = 5^2$
 $16 + 9 = 25$
b) 8·66 cm

Trigonometry in right-angled triangles (pages 64–65)

Box Q

1
a) 23·6°
b) 50·2°
c) 31·9°
d) 27·8°
e) 34·8°

2
a) 6 cm
b) 6·36 cm
c) 11·49 cm
d) 5·20 cm
e) 13·86 cm
f) 26·31 cm

3 28·5°

4 9·2 m

Box S

1
a) 9·8 km (1 d.p.)
b) 057° (nearest degree)

2 5·9° (1 d.p.)

3 66·4° (1 d.p.)

4 28·3 cm (1 d.p.)

Measures and measurement (pages 66–67)

Box M

1 c
2 b
3 a
4 c
5 d

Box Q

1
a) 7000 m
b) 0·6 m
c) 5 m
d) 2·5 kg
e) 6000 kg
f) 2600 ml
g) 5·8 l
h) 0·53 kg

2 Approx. 1.1 gallon

3 44·4 mph

4 1 hour 30 minutes

5 22 miles

6
Lower limit 15·75
Upper limit 15·85

7 $12·55 \leq h < 12·65$

Box S

1 32 km

2 James has the most sweets because 3 ounces is approximately 75 g.

3 13 g/cm³

4 98 miles

5
a) 25·5 metres
b) 12·25 metres
c) 54

Similarity (pages 68–69)

Box Q

1 Rectangles A and C

2
a) 3·65 cm
b) 4·98 cm

3
a) 6·1 cm
b) 11·5 cm
c) 10·7 cm
d) 3·6 cm

4
a) True
b) True

Box S

1
a) 30 cm
b) Ratio of widths   15 : 25
   = 3 : 5
   Capacity ratio   = 3³ : 5³
   = 27 : 125

2
a) $y = 10$ cm
b) $p = 8$ cm
c) No – because they only have one common angle of 110°:
 $(110° + 30° + 40°)$
 other $(110° + 50° + 20°)$

Area and perimeter of 2D shapes (pages 70–71)

Box Q

1
a) P = 12 cm; A = 6 cm²
b) P = 20·57 cm;
  A = 25·13 cm²
c) P = 25·13 cm;
  A = 50·27 cm²
d) P = 46·8 cm; A = 61·09 cm²

2
a) 122·5 cm²
b) 63·6 cm²

3
a) 15·7 m
b) 19·6 m²

4
320 cm²

Box S

1
a) 4 cm
b) 5 cm

2
a) 1256·6 cm²
b) 1570·8 cm²

3
a) 21·935 cm²
b) 0·0021935 m²

Volume of 3D solids (pages 72–73)

Box M

1 a
2 c
3 c
4 a

Box Q

1 10·8 cm³
2 682·5 cm³
3 1·94 m³ or 1 940 000 cm³
4 275 cm³
5 $\frac{4}{5}pq^2$, $\pi p^2 q$, $\frac{5}{6}pqr$

Box S

1 8·1 m

2
a) 198 cm³
b) 1584 cm³

7 $4\pi r2$ is a formula for area. 4π is a number and has no effect. r^2 means length × length which gives area. You would need to multiply by another length to get volume.

Collecting data (pages 74–75)

Box M

1 b
2 c
3 d

Box Q

1

Eye colour	Tally	Frequency

2 The tick boxes overlap; for example, in which box would somebody who watched 2 hours of television tick? Timescale? Is it per day? Per week? Need an extra box with 5 or more hours:

How much television do you watch per day?

less than 1 hr	1 up to 2 hrs	2 up to 3 hrs	3 up to 4 hrs

5

```
4 | 2  8  7  2  4
5 | 4  3  0  6  4  9
6 | 1  7  3  9
7 | 3  1  1
```

reordered =>

```
4 | 2  2  4  7  8
5 | 0  3  4  4  6  9
6 | 1  3  7  9
7 | 1  1  3
```

Box S

1

Weight (w) in grams	Frequency
$0 \leq w < 5$	4
$5 \leq w < 10$	2
$10 \leq w < 15$	7
$15 \leq w < 20$	4
$20 \leq w < 25$	5
$25 \leq w < 30$	6

2

a) The middle three boxes overlap with each other, for example: age 15 could be placed in two boxes.

b) less than 1 hour
1 up to 2 hours
2 up to 3 hours
3 hours and over

Representing data (pages 76–77)
Box Q

1

Day	1	2	3	4	5	6	7	8
Rainfall in mm	12	4	7	2	5	1	2	6

2

a) 120°

b) 8 hours

c) 6 hours

Box S

1

a)

b)

Time (t minutes)	Frequency
$0 \leq t < 5$	12
$5 \leq t < 10$	8
$10 \leq t < 15$	5
$15 \leq t < 20$	4
$20 \leq t < 25$	1

c) He is correct as two-thirds of the people queue for less than 10 minutes.

2

a)

b) $\frac{8}{24} = \frac{1}{3}$

Scatter diagrams and misleading graphs (pages 78–79)
Box Q

1

a) Graph X

b) Graph Z

c) Graph Y

d) Graph Y

e) Graph Z

2

a)

b) Positive correlation

c) See scatter diagram

d) 155·5 cm

Box S

1 The scale does not start at zero, so the growth looks much bigger than it actually is.

2

a) Positive correlation, the longer the hours spent revising the higher the maths score.

b) Negative correlation, the longer the hours spent watching the television, the lower the maths score.

c) Zero or no correlation.

d) Approx. 70%

Averages 1 (pages 80–81)
Box Q

1

a) 3·2

b) 2·5

c) 2

d) 6

2

32 cm

3

a) 24·75

b) Yes, as the mean is approximately 25.

4 She found the middle card but she did not put them in order of size first.

Box S

1

a) 8

b) (i) 9
(ii) 8
(iii) 9

2 7, 7, 13

3

a) 1·9

b) mode = 2, median = 2

Averages 2 (pages 82–83)
Box M

1 a
2 b
3 b
4 c

Box Q

1

a) True

b) False

c) True

d) True

e) False

f) False

Box S

1

a) 35 minutes

b) $30 \leq t < 40$

c) 11·3 minutes

d) $10 \leq t < 15$

e) The second set of students did the test in a quicker time, because the mean time was 11·3 minutes compared to 35 minutes for the first group.

2 Company B. The mean length was the same but the range was much smaller, hence the nails were probably more consistent in length.

Cumulative frequency graphs (pages 84–85)
Box Q

1

a) Median "approx" 54

b) Lower quartile "approx" 38

c) Upper quartile "approx" 59

d) Interquartile range "approx" 21

2

a)

Time in minutes	Frequency frequency	Cumulative
$0 \leq t < 10$	5	5
$10 \leq t < 20$	20	25
$20 \leq t < 30$	26	51
$30 \leq t < 40$	18	69
$40 \leq t < 50$	10	79
$50 \leq t < 60$	4	83

b)

c) Approx. 26 minutes

d) Interquartile range ≈18 minutes

e) About 8 people

Box S

1

a) Approx. £21

b) Approx. 68%

c) Approx. £10

d)

e) A ✓
B ✗
C ✗

Probability 1 (pages 86–87)
Box Q

1

a) $\frac{3}{13}$

b) $\frac{6}{13}$

c) 0

d) $\frac{7}{13}$

2

a) $\frac{15}{28}$

b) $\frac{13}{28}$

c) 0

3

a) True

b) False

c) False

4 140 people

5 42 races

Box S

1

a) Spinner Y, because 3 occupies two of the spaces and not just one as on spinner X.

b) Spinner X, because $\frac{3}{4}$ of the spinner has even numbers.

2

a) 0·15

b) Tomato

c) 0·4

d) 58%

e) 90 packets

Probability 2 (pages 88–89)
Box Q

1

a) $\frac{31}{150}$

b) Approach the expected probability of $\frac{1}{6}$

2

		Die					
		1	2	3	4	5	6
Coin	H	H1	H2	H3	H4	H5	H6
	T	T1	T2	T3	T4	T5	T6

b) $\frac{1}{12}$ c) $\frac{3}{12} = \frac{1}{4}$

3

a)

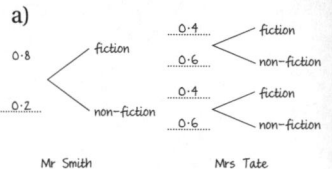

b) 0·32

c) 0·56

Box S

1

a) $\frac{7}{16}$

b) $\frac{10}{16}$

2

a) 6 races

b) 20 races

c) (i) 0·36
(ii) 0·48

SATs Exam Papers

Non-calculator paper

1
a) $a = 52°$
   $b = 76°$
   $c = 60°$
   $d = 30°$
   $e = 30°$

2
a) i) 1^4
   ii) 4^2
b) 2^4 3^4 4^6

3
a) $3n - 2$
b) $n^2 - 2$ or equivalent
c) $4y + 10 < 30$
d) $y < 5$
e) Javed is incorrect because $y < 5$, i.e. it can never be equal to 5.

4
a) $3\,cm$
b) $6\cdot\dot{6}\,cm$
c) The length of the larger rectangle is 4 times the length of the smaller rectangle. To be similar the widths must be in the same proportion but the width of the larger rectangle is only 3 times that of the smaller one. Ratio of sides $\frac{5}{4} \neq \frac{20}{12}$

5
a) $3\cdot2 \times 10^4$
b) $3000 = 3 \times 10^3$
c) $9\cdot28 \times 10^8$

6
a) $(3x \times 2x) + (2x \times 4y)$
   Area $= 6x^2 + 8xy$
b) V = area × depth
   $4x^2(3x + 4y) = 12x^3 + 16x^2y$
   depth $= 2x$

Calculator paper

1
a) i) $2n + 2s$
   ii) $4n + 2e + 6$
   iii) $5b + 2c + 2e$
b) $y = 4\,cm$

2
a) 20%
b) $\frac{12}{30} = \frac{2}{5}$ pupils
c)

	Skating	Cinema	Bowling
Number of pupils	3	15	12

d) 1 : 5 : 4
e) $\frac{3}{30} = \frac{1}{10}$

3
a) $4n + 5$
b) 32 cards

4
a) The older the car becomes the lower the value, or it has negative correlation.
b) £2250 – £3250
c) It may have been involved in a crash, may be damaged or badly rusted etc.
d) Between 5 and 6 years old.
e) A line which goes through the middle of the points with an approximately equal number on either side is acceptable.

5
a) See graph

b) See graph
c) The $2x$ helps decide if they are parallel, since 2 is the gradient of each line.
d) $y = 2x - 4$ etc. (any line as long as $2x$ forms part of the equation).
e) The constant, e.g. '+1' in $y = 2x + 1$ (any indication of the constant).
f) $(0, -10)$

6
a) Area $= 38\cdot465$
   $= 38\cdot47\,m^2$ (2 d.p.)
b) Height $= 7\cdot5\,m$
c) Area of grass $= 108\cdot04\,m^2$ (2 d.p.)
d) $28\cdot56\,m^3$
e) 24 white roses

7
a) Mean = 28 marks
b) 9A had a smaller average but a much higher range. This indicates that some students in 9A could have achieved higher marks than students in 9B. 9B's marks were more consistent than 9A's, hence the lower range and the higher average.

8
a) 10 km
b) 6 km
c) 11·7 km (1 d.p.)
d) See diagram

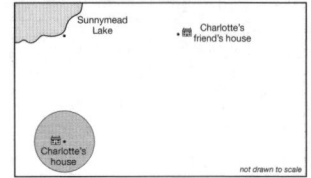

9
a) 18·6 (1 d.p.)
b) 40·4° (1 d.p.)

10
a)

Time (t minutes)	Frequency	Cumulative frequency
$0 \leq t < 2$	4	4
$2 \leq t < 4$	12	16
$4 \leq t < 6$	20	36
$6 \leq t < 8$	10	46
$8 \leq t < 210$	4	50

b)

c) 4·9 minutes (approximately)
d) 2·6 minutes (approximately)

LETTS EDUCATIONAL

The Chiswick Centre
414 Chiswick High Road
London W4 5TF
Tel: 020 8996 3333
Fax: 020 8742 8390
Email: mail@lettsed.co.uk
Website: www.letts-education.com

ISBN 1-84085-954-7

9 781840 859546

S These are SATs-style questions. Answer all parts of the questions.

1 Jeremy is making a box to hold a small chocolate egg.

He decides to draw a sketch of the net of the box.
The base of the box is shaded.

a) Complete the sketch of the net of the box. (1 mark)

b) Jacqueline is also making a box to hold a small chocolate egg.
   Her box has no lid.
   On a separate piece of paper,
   accurately draw a net for the box.

(3 marks)

2 This diagram shows a model made
  from 9 cubes. The cubes are either
  mauve or white. There are five mauve
  cubes and four white cubes.

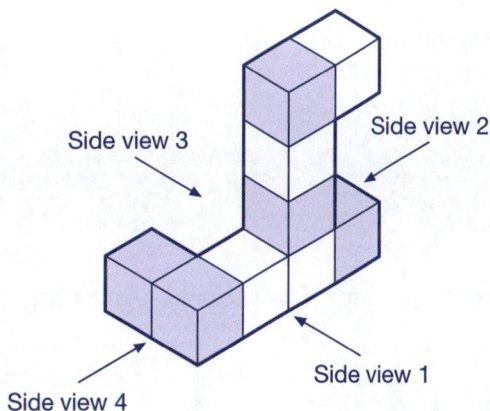

a) The drawings below show the side views of the model. Write the numbers to show
   which side view each drawing represents.

a)

b)

c)

d)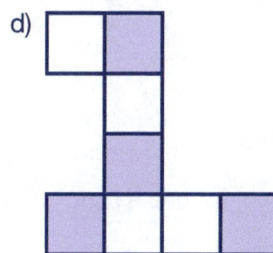

Side view . . . . . .   Side view . . . . .   Side view . . . . .   Side view . . . . . .

(2 marks)

b) On a separate piece of paper, draw the top view of the model, (2 marks)
   making sure you shade the mauve cubes.

Score .... /8

TOTAL SCORE   /18

For more help on this topic see KS3 Maths Success Guide pages 52–53

SYMMETRY

M Choose just one answer, A, B, C or D.

1 How many lines of symmetry does a rectangle have?
   a) 6 b) 4 c) 2 d) 8   (1 mark)

2 How many lines of symmetry does an isosceles triangle have?
   a) 3 b) 2 c) 1 d) 0   (1 mark)

3 What is the order of rotational symmetry of a square?
   a) 1 b) 2 c) 3 d) 4   (1 mark)

4 What is the order of rotational symmetry of this shape?

   a) 4 b) 2 c) 1 d) 3   (1 mark)

   Score .... /4

Q Answer all parts of all questions.

1 Complete the drawing so that the dotted line is a line of symmetry.

                                             (1 mark)

2 Write down the order of rotational symmetry, if any, of these shapes.

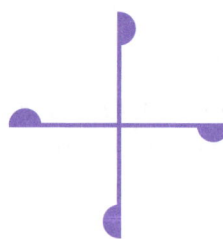

   a) ....   b) ....   c) ....   (3 marks)

3 Draw in one plane of symmetry on each of the shapes below.

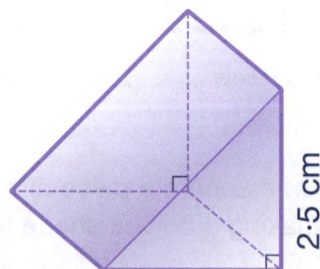

   2·5 cm

   2·5 cm

   a)   b)   c)   (3 marks)

   Score .... /7

These are SATs-style questions. Answer all parts of the questions.

1   Here are some shapes:

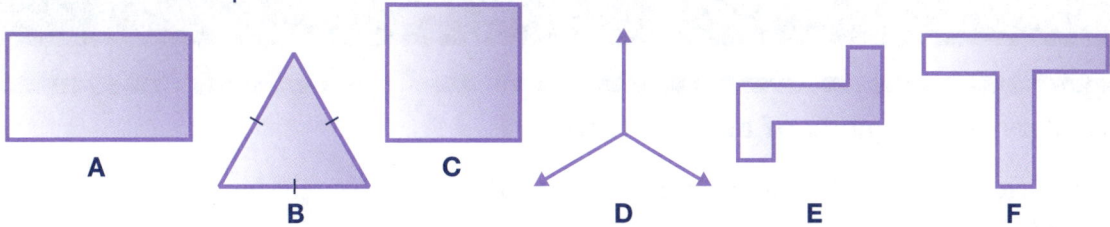

Write the letter of each shape in the correct space in the table below.
Shape C has been done for you.

<table>
<tr><td rowspan="2">Order of rotational symmetry</td><td colspan="6">Number of lines of symmetry</td></tr>
<tr><td></td><td>0</td><td>1</td><td>2</td><td>3</td><td>4</td></tr>
<tr><td></td><td>1</td><td></td><td></td><td></td><td></td><td></td></tr>
<tr><td></td><td>2</td><td></td><td></td><td></td><td></td><td></td></tr>
<tr><td></td><td>3</td><td></td><td></td><td></td><td></td><td></td></tr>
<tr><td></td><td>4</td><td></td><td></td><td></td><td></td><td>C</td></tr>
</table>

(5 marks)

2   a) The dotted lines
      are lines of symmetry.
      Complete each shape
      so that it is symmetrical.

(2 marks)

   b) This shape has two lines
      of symmetry.
      Complete the shape.

(4 marks)

3   This 3D shape has some planes of symmetry.

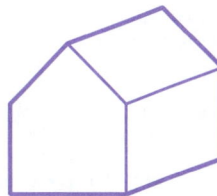

   a) How many planes of symmetry does this shape have?..(1 mark)

   b) Draw in one plane of symmetry on the shape.   (1 mark)

Score .... /13

TOTAL SCORE   /24

For more help on this topic see KS3 Maths Success Guide page 54

Q **Answer all parts of all questions.**

1 Here is a computer program to draw a triangle:

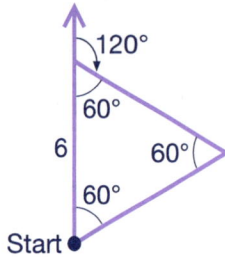

Forward 6
Turn right 120°

Forward......................

....

....

Complete the instructions to draw this shape.

(1 mark)

2 Use a ruler and compasses to draw an accurate diagram of the following shapes on a separate piece of paper.

a)

(2 marks)

b)

(2 marks)

3 Use a ruler and a protractor to draw the following shapes on a separate piece of paper.

a)

(1 mark)

b)

(1 mark)

c)

(1 mark)

4 Construct the perpendicular bisector of this line AB.

(2 marks)

5 Using compasses only, bisect this angle.

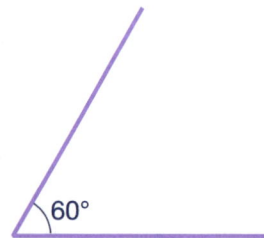

(2 marks)

Score .... /12

These are SATs-style questions. Answer all parts of the questions.

1   Shape A is a square.

The instructions to draw shape A are:

Forward 4

Turn right 90°

Forward 4

Turn right 90°

Forward 4

Turn right 90°

Forward 4

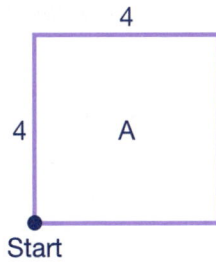

a) Write down the instructions to draw a square that has sides three times the length of those of shape A.

....

....

....(2 marks)

b) Shape B is a parallelogram.

Complete the instructions to draw shape B.

Forward 5

Turn right 60°

....

....

....

....

(2 marks)

2   Joshua has made a rough sketch of this triangle.

Using compasses, construct the triangle accurately in the space provided.

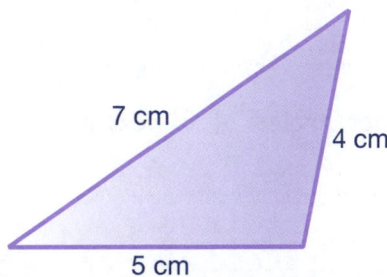

(2 marks)

Score .... /6

TOTAL SCORE   /18

For more help on this topic see KS3 Maths Success Guide page 55

Q Answer all parts of all questions.

1 Work out the size of the angle a in each of the diagrams.

a)

b)

c)

a = ...

a = ...

a = ...

d)

e)

f)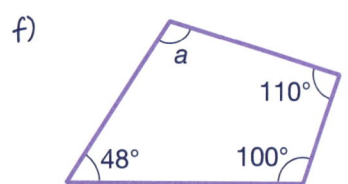

a = ...

a = ...

a = ... (6 marks)

2 Calculate the size of the angles marked with letters.

a)

b)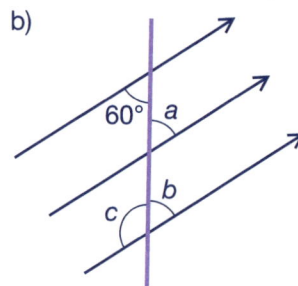

a) a = ...   b = ...   c = ...

b) a = ...   b = ...   c = ... (6 marks)

3 The size of an exterior angle of a regular polygon is 18°. How many sides does the polygon have?

....(1 mark)

4 Calculate the sum of the interior angles of a hexagon.

....(1 mark)

5 Add six more shapes to this tessellation.

(2 marks)

Score .... /16

These are SATs-style questions. Answer all parts of the questions.

1 a) Fiona has drawn a shape
        using her computer.

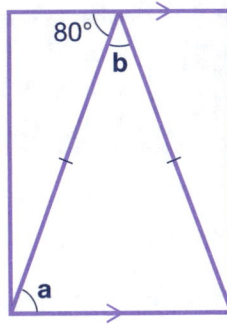

80°

b

a

The diagram shows an isosceles triangle inside a rectangle.

   i) Calculate the size of the angle marked **a**.   **a** = ... °   (1 mark)

   ii) Calculate the size of the angle marked **b**.   **b** = ... °   (1 mark)

   b) Simon has drawn this shape
        with his computer.

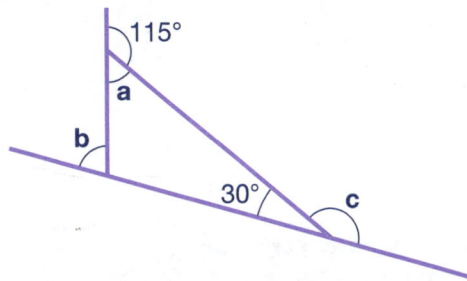

115°

a

b

30°   **c**

Calculate angles **a**, **b** and **c**.
Show your working.

   a = ...   **b** = ...   **c** = ...   (3 marks)

   c) Simon draws a second shape
        with his computer.

a   **b**

It is a regular hexagon.

   i) Calculate the sizes of angles **a** and **b**.
        Show your working.

   a = ...   **b** = ...   (2 marks)

   ii) Explain why a regular hexagon will tessellate.

   ....

   ....(1 mark)

   Score .... /8

TOTAL SCORE   /24

BEARINGS AND SCALE DRAWINGS

Q   **Answer all parts of all questions.**

1 Calculate the three-figure bearing of: i) B from A and ii) A from B in each diagram.

   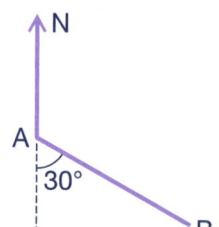

a) ....

....

b) ....

....

c) ....

....

d) ....

....

(8 marks)

2 Preachers Bottom is 8 km due north of Hookfield. Marigold Hill is on a bearing of 060° from Hookfield, whilst it is on a bearing of 110° from Preachers Bottom.

Make a careful scale drawing, using a scale of 1 cm to 1 km and find the distance of Marigold Hill from Hookfield.

Measure the bearing of Hookfield from Marigold Hill.

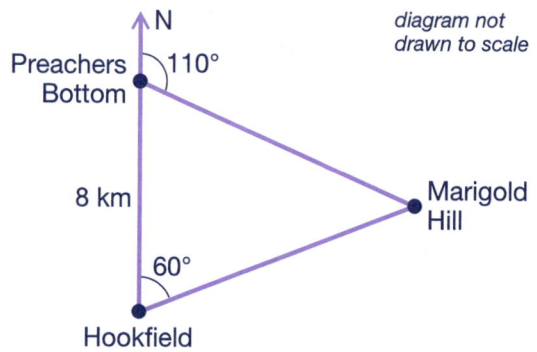

diagram not drawn to scale

(3 marks)

3 The scale on a road map is 1:50 000. If two towns are 20 cm apart on the map, work out the real distance, in kilometres, between the two towns.

....(2 marks)

Score .... /13

These are SATs-style questions. Answer all parts of the questions.

1   Yen is making a stencil.
    He makes a sketch of the
    stencil on some paper.

    A _____ B
    4·6 cm ⌐100°   110°⌐ 5·2 cm
         C   6 cm   D

   a) Make an accurate full-size drawing of the stencil in the space provided.

                                                                      (4 marks)

   b) Measure the length of AB to the nearest 0·1 cm.   .... cm   (1 mark)

2   a) The diagram shows the position of a lighthouse (L). A ship (S) is 120 km from the
       lighthouse on a bearing of 140°. If 1 cm = 20 km, mark accurately on the diagram
       the position of the ship.

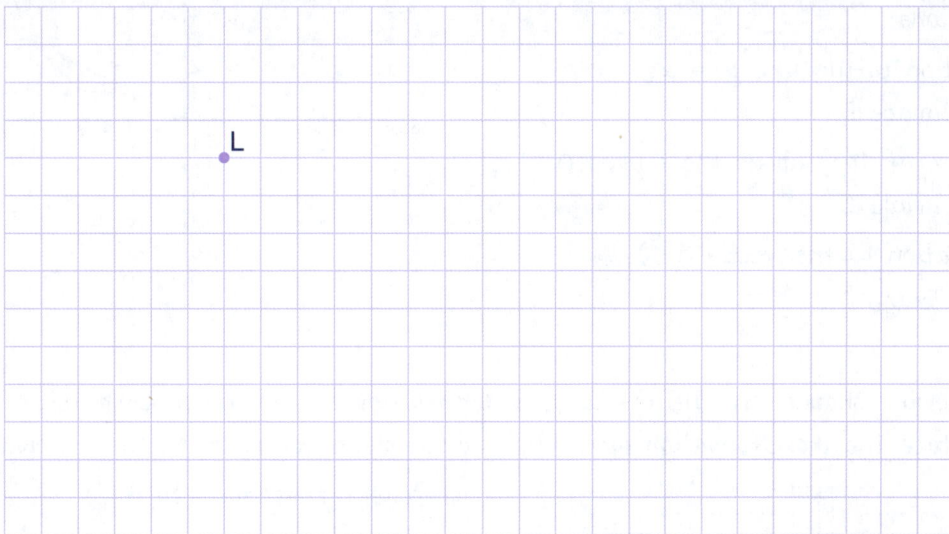

                                                                      (3 marks)

   b) A buoy (B) is 80 km and on a bearing of 040° from the ship. Mark accurately
      on the diagram the position of the buoy.   (2 marks)

   c) How far is the lighthouse from the buoy?   .... km   (1 mark)

   Score .... /11

TOTAL SCORE   /24

For more help on this topic see KS3 Maths Success Guide pages 58–59

TRANSFORMATIONS

M Choose just one answer, a, b, c or d.

Questions 1–3 refer to the diagram below.

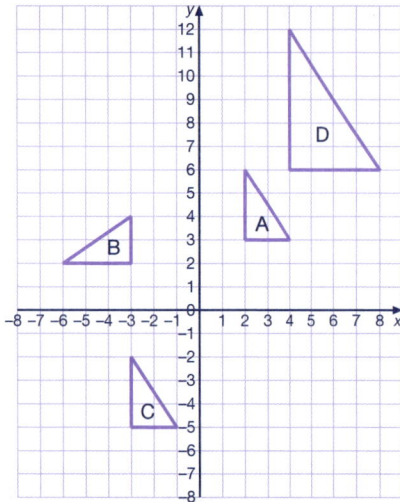

1 What is the transformation that would map shape A onto shape B?
a) reflection b) rotation c) translation
d) enlargement   (1 mark)

2 What is the transformation that would map shape A onto shape C?
a) reflection b) rotation c) translation
d) enlargement   (1 mark)

3 What is the transformation that would map shape A onto shape D?
a) reflection b) rotation c) translation
d) enlargement   (1 mark)

Score .... /3

Q Answer all parts of all questions.

1 On the grid opposite, draw the image of the shaded shape after the following transformations:

a) a reflection in the line y = x;
call the image B

b) a rotation of 180° about the origin (0, 0);
call the image C

c) a translation by the vector $\binom{-5}{4}$;
call the image D.

(3 marks)

2 All the following shapes are the result of a translation, a reflection, or a rotation of object A. State the transformation which has taken place for each of the following:

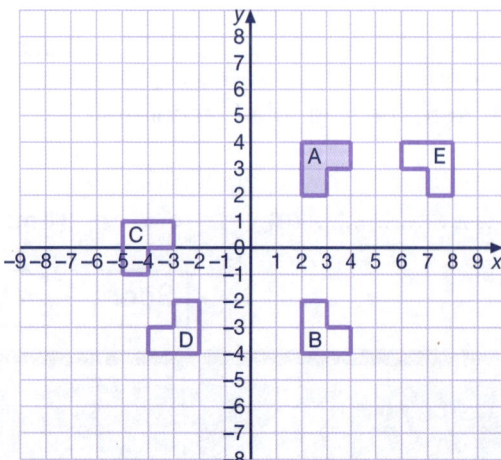

a) A is transformed to B

....(1 mark)

b) A is transformed to C

....(1 mark)

c) A is transformed to D

....(1 mark)

d) A is transformed to E

....(1 mark)

Score .... /7

These are SATs-style questions. Answer all parts of the questions.

1 Reflect triangle P in the mirror line on each of these diagrams.

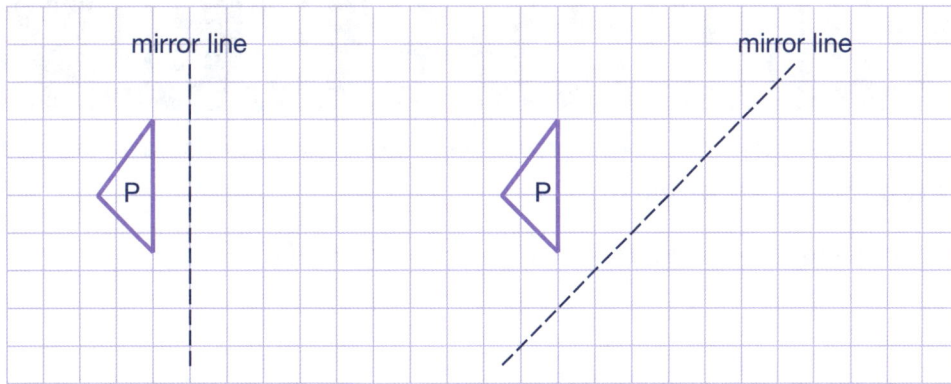

mirror line   mirror line

P   P

(2 marks)

2 Five cubes join together to make a ☐ shape.
The diagram shows the ☐ shape after quarter turns in one direction.
On the paper below, draw the ☐ shape after the next quarter turn in the same direction.

(2 marks)

3 a) The grid shows a T shape. On the grid draw an enlargement of scale factor 2 of the T shape. Use point Y as the centre of enlargement.

Y•

(2 marks)

b) This sketch shows two rectangles. The bigger rectangle is an enlargement of scale factor 2·5 of the smaller rectangle. Write down the two missing values.

5 cm

......

......

9 cm

(2 marks)

Score .... /8

TOTAL SCORE   /18

For more help on this topic see KS3 Maths Success Guide pages 60–61

LOCI AND COORDINATES IN 3D

Q **Answer all parts of all questions.**

For each of the statements below, decide whether it is true or false.

1

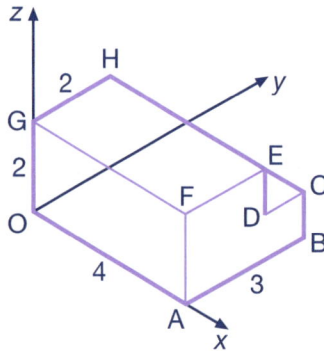

a) The coordinates of point A are (4, 0, 0)..(1 mark)

b) The coordinates of point H are (0, 2, 2)..(1 mark)

c) The coordinates of point E are (2, 4, 2)..(1 mark)

d) The coordinates of point C are (4, 3, 1)..(1 mark)

2 Tess buries her bone in the garden. The garden is surrounded by a fence ABCD, as shown.

i) The bone is buried at least 2 metres from the greenhouse.

ii) The bone is buried at least 3 metres from the centre of the pond (P).

iii) The bone is buried at least 1 metre from the house.

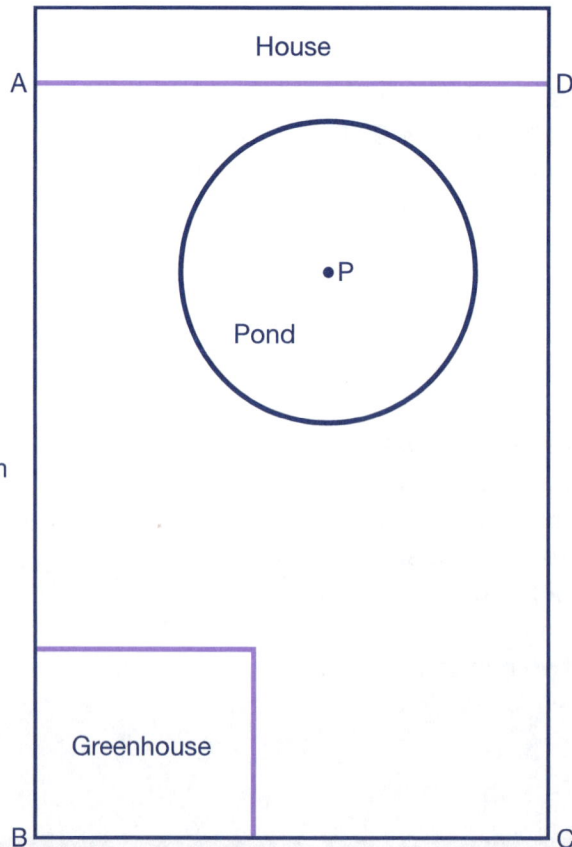

Scale 1 cm = 1 m

Shade in all the possible areas where Tess could have buried her bone.

(4 marks)

Score .... /8

These are SATs-style questions. Answer all parts of the questions.

1   The diagram shows the positions
    of three towns, C, D and E.

    A supermarket (S) is to be built so that it is:

    i)   equidistant from D and E

    ii) 12 km from town C.

    By drawing the loci of i) and ii) and using
    a scale of 1 cm = 4 km, clearly mark the
    position of the supermarket.

    N

    C

    D

    E   (3 marks)

2   In the scale drawing below, the shaded area represents a fish pond.
    There is a wire fence all around the pond.
    The shortest distance from the fence to the edge of the pond is always 2 m.

    On the diagram, draw accurately the position of the fence.

    1 m
    1 m

    Scale 5 mm = 1 m   (3 marks)

3   The diagram shows a solid.
    Complete the coordinates for
    each of the vertices listed below.

    R = (..............., ..., ...)

    S = (..............., ..., ...)

    T = (..............., ..., ...)

    y

    T

    S

    U

    1 cm   1 cm   R

    3 cm   3 cm

    z

    3 cm

    x

                                                         (3 marks)

    Score .... /9

For more help on this topic see KS3 Maths Success Guide page 62

PYTHAGORAS' THEOREM

Q Answer all parts of all questions.

1 Giovanna is playing a game. She writes the missing lengths of some triangles onto cards.

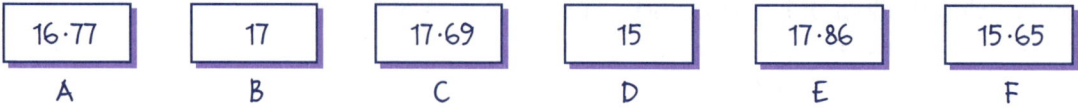

| 16·77 | 17 | 17·69 | 15 | 17·86 | 15·65 |
| A | B | C | D | E | F |

Match each length with the correct triangle.

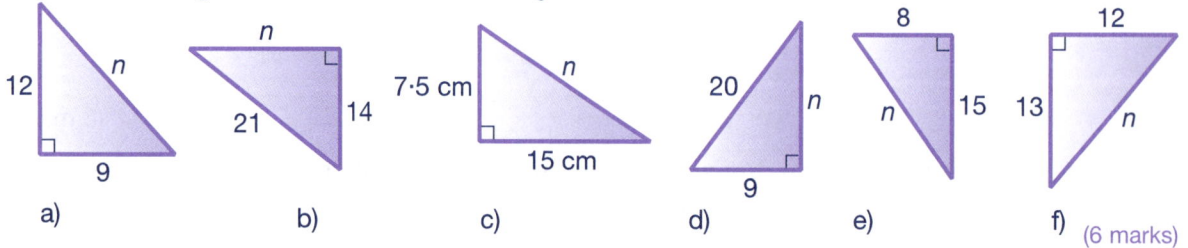

a) b) c) d) e) f)

(6 marks)

2 Hannah says:

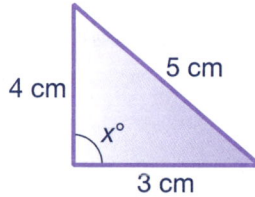

Angle x must be 90°.

Explain how Hannah knows this without measuring the size of the angle.

....

....(2 marks)

3 Calculate the distances of these lines:

a) RS ....

b) VW ....

c) XY ....

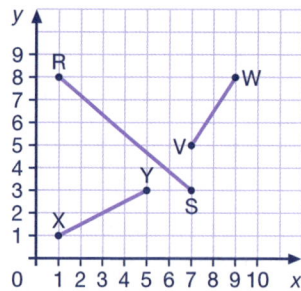

(3 marks)

4 Calculate the length of the diagonal of this rectangle.
Give your answer to 1 decimal place.

22·3 cm

9·2 cm

.... (2 marks)

5 Calculate the perpendicular height of this isosceles triangle.
Give your answer to 1 decimal place.

15 m   15 m

12 m

.... (2 marks)

Score .... /15

S These are SATs-style questions. Answer all parts of the questions.

1   A ship sails from Miami to an island in the Atlantic. The island is 300 km North of Miami and 450 km East of Miami.
Calculate the shortest distance
between the island and Miami.

Island

Miami

Sea

not to scale

Show your working...(3 marks)

2   Look at this triangle.
Without measuring, explain why
angle p must be a right angle.

15 cm   17 cm

$p°$

8 cm

Show your working. ....

....

....(2 marks)

3   The cross-section of a triangular prism is a right-angled triangle.

Calculate the height (n) of the triangle.
Give your answer to 1 decimal place.
Show full working out.

22 cm

n

16 cm

....(2 marks)

4   PQR and RSP are both right-angled triangles.

R

4 cm   S

Q

3 cm   10 cm

P

a) Explain why the length of RP is 5 cm.

....(1 mark)

b) Calculate the length of RS.

Show your working...(2 marks)

Score .... /10

TOTAL SCORE   /25

For more help on this topic see KS3 Maths Success Guide page 63

TRIGONOMETRY IN RIGHT-ANGLED TRIANGLES

Q Answer all parts of all questions.

1 Calculate the size of the unknown angle in each of these triangles. Give your answers to 1 decimal place.

10 cm / 4 cm / θ

25 cm / 16 cm / θ

37 cm / 23 cm / θ

15 cm / 7 cm / θ

36 cm / 25 cm / θ

a) ....   b) ....   c) ....   d) ....   e) .... (5 marks)

2 Calculate the length of side x in each of the triangles below. Give your answers to 2 decimal places, where necessary.

x / 12 cm / 30°

x / 45° / 9 cm

x / 50° / 15 cm / x

x / 30° / 9 cm

x / 60° / 12 cm

x / 70° / 9 cm

a) ....   b) ....   c) ....   d) ....   e) ....   f) ....

(6 marks)

3 A tower of height 25 metres casts a shadow of length 46 metres on horizontal ground.

Calculate the angle of elevation of the sun. Give your answer to 1 decimal place.

25 metres

46 metres

....(2 marks)

4 A ladder of length 12 metres rests against a wall in such a way that the angle the ladder makes with the wall is 40°.

Calculate the height of the top of the ladder above the ground, giving your answer to 1 decimal place.

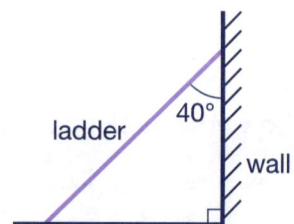

40°

ladder

wall

....(2 marks)

Score .... /15

1 Eagle Point is 8·2 km East and 5·4 km North of Briarton.

not to scale

a) Calculate the direct distance from Briarton to Eagle Point.

Show your working..(2 marks)

b) Ellen wants to sail directly from Briarton to Eagle Point. On what bearing should she sail?

Show your working..(2 marks)

2 DEF and DFG are both right-angled triangles:

not drawn accurately

By how many degrees is angle *p* bigger than angle *q*?

Show your working...degrees   (4 marks)

3 Calculate the size of angle *m* in this isosceles triangle.

not drawn accurately

Show your working.   *m* = ...(2 marks)

4 Calculate the perimeter of this triangle. Give your answer to 1 decimal place.

Show your working. perimeter =...(3 marks)

Score .... /13

MEASURES AND MEASUREMENT

M Choose just one answer, a, b, c or d.

1 How many millimetres are in 5·2 cm?
a) 0·52 mm b) 5200 mm c) 52 mm d) 520 mm
(1 mark)

2 Approximately how many pounds are in 3 kg?
a) 4·5 b) 6·6 c) 5·8 d) 9
(1 mark)

3 Nigel is 175 cm tall. What is the lower limit of his height?
a) 174·5 cm b) 175 cm c) 175·5 cm d) 174·9 cm
(1 mark)

4 A car travels 150 km in 1 hour and 20 minutes. What is the average speed of the car in km per hour?
a) 100 b) 125 c) 112·5 d) 120
(1 mark)

5 What is the volume of a piece of wood with a density of 680 kg/m³ and a mass of 34 kg?
a) 0·5 m³ b) 20 m³ c) 2 m³ d) 0·05 m³
(1 mark)

Score .... /5

Q Answer all parts of all questions.

1 Complete the statements below.

a) 7 km = ...m

b) 60 cm = ...m

c) 500 mm = ...m

d) 2500 g = ...kg

e) 6 tonnes = ...kg

f) 2·6 l = ...ml

g) 580 cl = ...l

h) 530 g = ...kg
(8 marks)

2 A container holds 5 litres of water.
Approximately how many gallons is this?...(1 mark)

3 Joanne drove 200 miles in 4 hours and 30 minutes.
At what average speed did she travel?...(2 marks)

4 Tracey drove 90 miles at an average speed of 60 mph.
How long did it take her?...(2 marks)

5 How far does Ahmed walk if he walks at a speed of 4 miles per hour for 5 hours and 30 minutes?

....(2 marks)

6 Thomas runs a race. His time is 15·8 seconds to the nearest tenth of a second.
Write down the upper and lower limits of his time...(2 marks)

7 The height (*h*) of a plant is 12·6 cm to the nearest tenth of a centimetre. Complete this inequality which shows the values between which the height of the plant can lie.

$12·55 \leq h < 12·$...(1 mark)

Score .... /18

These are SATs-style questions. Answer all parts of the questions.

1   How many kilometres are there
    in 20 miles?
    Complete the missing part of this sign.

Bridleway to Swanmore
20 miles or . . . . . kilometres

(1 mark)

2   Jessica and James have some sweets.

I have 50 g of sweets.

Jessica

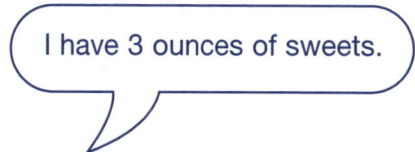

I have 3 ounces of sweets.

James

Who has the most sweets?
Explain your answer. ....(2 marks)

3   The mass of a toy is 650 g. If the volume of the toy is 50 cm³, work out the toy's density.

    ....(2 marks)

4   A bus travels for $3\frac{1}{2}$ hours at an average speed of 28 mph. How far does the bus travel?

    ....(1 mark)

5   A flower garden has
    been marked out as
    shown in the diagram.

26 metres

not to
scale

flower garden

12·3 metres

a) The length of the flower garden is 26 metres, to the nearest metre.
    What is the shortest possible length of the flower garden?

    .... m   (1 mark)

b) The width of the flower garden is 12·3 metres to the nearest tenth of a metre.
    What is the shortest possible width of the flower garden?

    ....(1 mark)

c) Fifty rose bushes (to the nearest ten) are planted in the garden.
    What is the maximum number of rose bushes that are planted?

    ....(1 mark)

Score .... /9

TOTAL SCORE   /32

For more help on this topic see KS3 Maths Success Guide pages 66–68

SIMILARITY

Q **Answer all parts of all questions.**

1 Here are three rectangles. Which two are similar?

diagrams not drawn to scale

....(1 mark)

2 Triangle PQR is similar to triangle MNO.
Angle PQR = Angle MNO
Angle PRQ = Angle MON

diagrams not drawn to scale

a) Calculate the length of PR, giving your answer to 3 s.f. ....cm (2 marks)

b) Calculate the length of MN, giving your answer to 3 s.f. ....cm (2 marks)

3 Calculate the lengths marked x in these similar shapes. Give your answers correct to 1 decimal place.

a)

b)

x = ...

x = ...

c)

d)

x = ...

x = ...   (8 marks)

4 Decide whether these statements are true or false.

a) If two shapes are similar, corresponding sides are in the same ratio. ....

b) If two shapes are similar, corresponding angles are the same. ....

(2 marks)

Score .... /15

These are SATs-style questions. Answer all parts of the questions.

1 These vases are mathematically similar.
The dimensions are shown.

not to scale

15 cm

25 cm

18 cm

n

a) Calculate the value of *n*.
Show your working.   *n* =.............................cm   **(2 marks)**

b) Think about the ratio of the widths of the two vases.
Explain why the ratio of the capacity of the smaller pot to the capacity of the larger pot is 27 : 125.

....**(1 mark)**

2 These triangles are similar.

6 cm

a

b

y

15 cm

b

a

9 cm

not to scale

a) What is the value of *y*?

Show your working.   *y* = ... cm   **(2 marks)**

b) Triangles ABC and BDE are similar.
What is the value of *p*?
Show your working.

not to scale

A

E

20 cm

p

C

D

B

12 cm

30 cm

p = ...cm   **(2 marks)**

c) Look at these triangles.
Are they similar?
Show your working.

110°

30°

50°

110°

....**(1 mark)**

Score .... /8

TOTAL SCORE   /23

For more help on this topic see KS3 Maths Success Guide page 69

S I M I L A R I T Y

69

AREA AND PERIMETER OF 2D SHAPES

Q   **Answer all parts of all questions.**

1 For each of these shapes, calculate a) the perimeter (P) and b) the area (A).

a)   b)   c)   d)

....(8 marks)

2 Work out the areas of these shapes. Give your answers to 1 decimal place.

a)   b)

....(4 marks)

3 A circular rose garden has a diameter of 5 m.

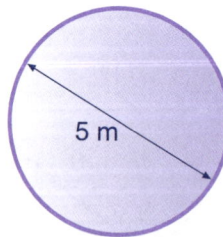

Find:

a) the circumference of the garden ....(1 mark)

b) the area of the garden ....(2 marks)

4 The area of a shape is 20 cm². The lengths of the shape are enlarged by a scale factor of 4. What is the area of the enlarged shape?

....(1 mark)

Score .... /16

These are SATs-style questions. Answer all parts of the questions.

1 Each shape in this question has an area of 20 cm^2.

a) Calculate the height of this rectangle.

area = 20 cm^2

height

5 cm

height = ... cm   (1 mark)

b) Calculate the height of this triangle.

area = 20 cm^2

height

8 cm

height = ... cm   (1 mark)

2 a) A circle has a radius of 20 cm.

20 cm

Calculate the area of the circle. Show your working.   ....cm^2 (2 marks)

b) A circle of radius 20 cm sits inside a circle of radius 30 cm. Calculate the area of the shaded region.

30 cm

20 cm

Show your working.   ....cm^2 (3 marks)

3 A sewing pattern is in the shape of a trapezium.

3·2 cm

4·1 cm

7·5 cm

a) Calculate the area of the trapezium. Show your working.   ....cm^2 (2 marks)

b) What is the area of the trapezium in square metres? ....m^2 (1 mark)

Score .... /10

TOTAL SCORE   /26

For more help on this topic see KS3 Maths Success Guide pages 70–71

VOLUME OF 3D SOLIDS

M Choose just one answer, a, b, c or d.

1 The volume of a cuboid is 20 cm³.
If the height is 1 cm and the width is 4 cm, what is the length?
a) 5 cm b) 10 cm c) 15 cm d) 8 cm (1 mark)

2 A cube of volume 2 cm³ is enlarged by a scale factor of 3.
What is the volume of the enlarged cube?
a) 6 cm b) 27 cm³ c) 54 cm³ d) 18 cm (1 mark)

3 The letter b represents a length. What does this formula represent? $\frac{4b^3}{\pi}$
a) length b) area c) volume d) nothing (1 mark)

4 The letters a and b represent lengths. What does this formula represent? $\sqrt{a^2 - b^2}$
a) length b) area c) volume d) nothing (1 mark)

Score .... /4

Q Answer all parts of all questions.

1 The diagram shows a triangular prism.
Work out the volume of the triangular prism, clearly stating your units.
Give your answer to 3 significant figures.

....

....

diagrams not drawn to scale

9 cm
0·2 m
12 cm

(2 marks)

2 The shape opposite is the cross-section of a prism, 15 cm long. Find the volume of the prism, clearly stating your units.

....

....

5 cm
6·5 cm
9 cm

(2 marks)

3 Calculate the volume of the oil drum, clearly stating your units.
Give your answer to 3 significant figures.

....

....

125 cm
EXPRESS OIL
1·58 m

(2 marks)

4 A child's toy is made up of a cuboid and a cylinder. Calculate the volume of the toy, giving your answer to 3 significant figures.

....

....

3 cm
5 cm
8 cm
6 cm
5 cm

(2 marks)

5 Here are some expressions.

$4\pi r^2$	$\frac{4}{5}pq^2$	$\sqrt{p^2 + q^2}$	$\pi p^2 q$	$\frac{5}{6}pqr$	$\frac{\pi p^2}{q}$

The letters p, q and r represent lengths.
π, 4, 5, 6 are numbers that have no dimensions.
Three of the expressions represent volume. Tick the boxes underneath
these expressions.

(3 marks)

Score .... /11

S These are SATs-style questions. Answer all parts of the questions.

1 Some plates are put into a box. There are two types of boxes. If the volume of each box is the same, calculate the missing height of box B.

4·5 m   height   *diagrams not drawn to scale*

A   6 m   B   2·5 m
3 m   4 m

....cm (3 marks)

2 A piece of cheese is in the shape of a triangular prism.

5·5 cm

6 cm

12 cm

a) Calculate the volume of the piece of cheese.

Show your working...cm³ (2 marks)

b) A larger block of cheese is exactly the same shape but each of the lengths is double that of the first piece of cheese.
Calculate the volume of the larger block of cheese.

Show your working...cm³ (2 marks)

3 Explain why the formula $4\pi r^2$, where r is a length, cannot be a formula for volume?

....(1 mark)

Score .... /8

TOTAL SCORE   /23

For more help on this topic see KS3 Maths Success Guide pages 72–73

VOLUME OF 3D SOLIDS

73

COLLECTING DATA

M — Choose just one answer, a, b, c or d.

Use the frequency table given to answer the next three questions.

Weight (kg)	Frequency
$40 \leq w < 50$	4
$50 \leq w < 60$	10
$60 \leq w < 70$	15
$70 \leq w < 80$	25
$80 \leq w < 90$	4

1 How many people had a weight between 50 and 60 kg?
a) 4 b) 10 c) 15 d) 25 (1 mark)

2 How many people in total were surveyed about their weight?
a) 55 b) 30 c) 58 d) 60 (1 mark)

3 If somebody weighed 70 kg, into which class interval would they go?
a) $40 \leq w < 50$ b) $50 \leq w < 60$ c) $60 \leq w < 70$
d) $70 \leq w < 80$ (1 mark)

Score .... /3

Q — Answer all parts of all questions.

1 Jerry and Kamaljeet are collecting some data on eye colour for a class survey. Design an observation sheet that they could use. (3 marks)

2 Joe and Rhysian are designing a survey to use in the school. One of their questions is shown below:

How much television do you watch per day?

0–1 hrs	1–2 hrs	2–3 hrs	3–4 hrs

What is the problem with this question? Rewrite the question so that it is improved.

....

....(2 marks)

3 The weights in kg of some students are:

42, 54, 61, 67, 53, 50, 48, 47, 56, 42, 44, 54, 59, 63, 73, 71, 69, 71

Complete the stem and leaf diagram below:

```
4 | 2   8   7   2   4
5 |
6 |
7 |
```

stem = 10 kg
key 4|2 means 42 (2 marks)

Score .... /7

These are SATs-style questions. Answer all parts of the questions.

1   The following data show the weights (w) in grams of some packets of sweets.

22	18	4	26	27	21	24
16	8	3	3	12	21	25
14	28	27	10	11	10	14
13	21	6	2	27	18	15

The data are placed into a frequency table. Complete the gaps in the table below.

Weight (w) in grams	Frequency
0 ≤ w < 5	4
5 ≤ w < 10	2
.... ≤ w < 15	....
15 ≤ w <	....
20 ≤ w < 25	....
.... ≤ w < 30	5

(3 marks)

2   Some pupils are doing a survey to find out the number of hours spent watching television in a week. They wrote a questionnaire.

a) One question was:
How old are you (in years)?

10 or younger   10 to 15   15 to 20   20 to 25   25 or older

Explain why the labels for the middle three boxes need to be changed.

....(2 marks)

b) Another question was:
How long do you spend watching television in a week?

☐ don't know   ☐ none   ☐ a small amount   ☐ lots

Jonathan said that the labels need changing.
Write new labels for the boxes. You may change as many boxes as you want.

....(2 marks)

Score .... /7

TOTAL SCORE   /17

For more help on this topic see KS3 Maths Success Guide pages 76–77

Q **Answer all parts of all questions.**

1 The number of millimetres of rainfall that fell during the first eight days of August are shown on the line graph below:

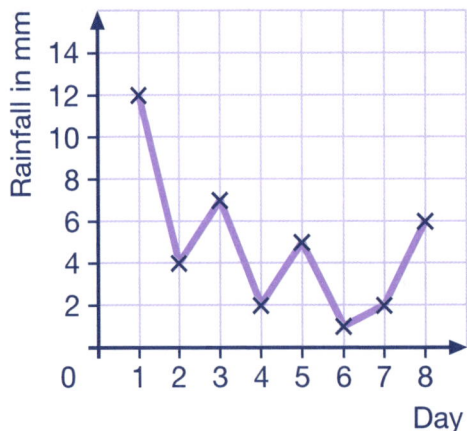

Using the information on the graph, complete the table below.

Day	1	2	3	4	5	6	7	8
Rainfall in mm		4				1		6

(2 marks)

2 The pie chart shows how Erin spends a typical day.

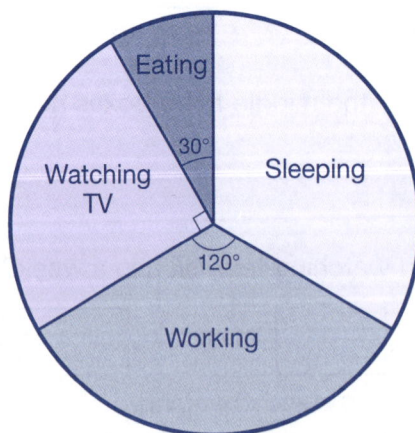

a) Measure the size of the angle for sleeping. ....

b) Work out the number of hours that Erin works. ....

c) For how many hours does Erin watch TV? ....

(3 marks)

Score .... /5

These are SATs-style questions. Answer all parts of the questions.

1 The frequency table and chart show how long (in minutes) 30 people spent queuing at a supermarket checkout.

Time (*t* minutes)	Frequency
0 ≤ t < 5	12
5 ≤ t < 10	....
10 ≤ t < 15	....
15 ≤ t < 20	4
20 ≤ t < 25	1

a) Use the information in the frequency table to complete the frequency diagram.   (2 marks)

b) Use the information in the frequency diagram to complete the frequency table.   (2 marks)

c) Rameen says:

> Most people queue for less than 10 minutes.

Explain whether he is right...(1 mark)

2 A teacher asked his class:

'What is your favourite type of take-away?'

a) The results are shown in the table below:

Type of take-away	Frequency
Indian	11
Chinese	4
Pizza	8
Fried chicken	1

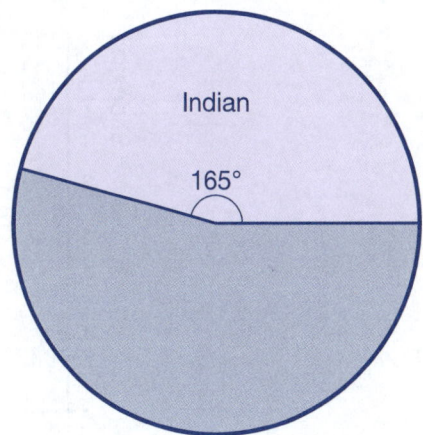

Complete the pie chart to show this information. Show your working and draw your angles accurately.

(2 marks)

b) What fraction of the students prefer pizza?

....(1 mark)

Score .... /8

TOTAL SCORE   /13

For more help on this topic see KS3 Maths Success Guide pages 78–79

Q **Answer all parts of all questions.**

1

Graph X

Graph Y

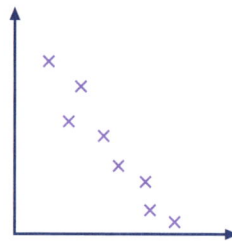
Graph Z

Which of the graphs above best illustrates the relationship between:

a) the weight of children and their mark in a maths test? Graph.................................(1 mark)

b) the age of a car and its value?   Graph.................................(1 mark)

c) the age of a car and its mileage?   Graph.................................(1 mark)

d) the temperature and the sales of ice cream?   Graph.................................(1 mark)

e) the temperature and the sales of woollen hats?   Graph.................................(1 mark)

2 In a survey, the heights of ten girls and their shoe sizes were measured.

Height in cm	150	157	159	161	158	164	154	152	162	168
Shoe size	3	5	$5\frac{1}{2}$	6	5	$6\frac{1}{2}$	4	$3\frac{1}{2}$	6	7

a) Draw a scatter diagram showing this data.

(2 marks)

b) What type of correlation is there between height and shoe size?

....(1 mark)

c) Draw a line of best fit on your diagram.   (1 mark)

d) From your scatter diagram, estimate the height of a girl whose shoe size is $4\frac{1}{2}$.

....(1 mark)

Score .... /10

These are SATs-style questions. Answer all parts of the questions.

1   The following graph shows the sales of some washing powder over a period of 4 months.

Explain why this graph is misleading. ....(2 marks)

2   Some students did a survey of how well they did in a maths test compared to the hours they spent revising and the hours spent watching television. They plotted their results as scatter diagrams.

a) What does Graph 1 show about the relationship between the maths percentage and the hours spent revising?

....(1 mark)

b) What does Graph 2 show about the relationship between the maths percentage and the hours spent watching television?

....(1 mark)

c) If a scatter diagram was drawn to show the relationship between the students' maths percentages and their heights, what type of correlation would it have?

....(1 mark)

d) Another student spent 3 hours revising. Using Graph 1, estimate the student's score in the maths test.

....(1 mark)

Score .... /6

TOTAL SCORE   /16

For more help on this topic see KS3 Maths Success Guide pages 80–81

AVERAGES 1

Q **Answer all parts of all questions.**

1 Here are some number cards:

| 2 | 7 | 3 | 6 | 2 | 2 | 1 | 3 | 4 | 2 |

For the numbers cards, calculate:

a) the mean ....(1 mark)

b) the median...(1 mark)

c) the mode..(1 mark)

d) the range..(1 mark)

2 The mean length of 10 tadpoles is 3·2 cm. What is the total length of the tadpoles in centimetres?

....(1 mark)

3 The Chunky Crisp Company claims that, 'On average, a packet of crisps contains 25 crisps.'

In order to check the accuracy, a sample of 20 packets were taken and the number of crisps in each bag counted.

Crisps	23	24	25	26	27
Number of packets	3	3	12	0	2

a) Find the mean number of crisps per bag in this sample.

....(2 marks)

b) Explain briefly whether you think the manufacturer is justified in making its claim.

....(1 mark)

4 Jessie finds the median of some cards:

| 7 | 2 | 9 | 4 | 10 |

She says that '9 is the median'. Explain why she is wrong.

....(2 marks)

Score .... /10

S **These are SATs-style questions. Answer all parts of the questions.**

1   Ellie has these four number cards:

| 1 | 9 | 4 | 2 |

The mean is 4.

a) What is the range of the numbers? ....(1 mark)

b) Ellie takes another card:

| 1 | 9 | 4 | 2 | ? |

The mean of the five cards is now 5.

i)   What number is on her new card?..(1 mark)

ii) What is the range of her cards now?..(1 mark)

iii) What is the mode of her five cards?...(1 mark)

2   There are three hidden cards.

| ? | ? | ? |

The mode of the three numbers is 7.
The mean of the three numbers is 9.

What are the three numbers? ....(3 marks)

3   In a Sunday league football tournament, the number of goals scored is shown in the table below.

Number of goals scored (x)	0	1	2	3	4	5
Frequency	5	8	9	3	3	2

a) Work out the mean number of goals scored in the tournament.

   ....(2 marks)

b Work out the mode and the median.

   mode = ...   median = ... (2 marks)

Score ...... /11

TOTAL SCORE   /21

For more help on this topic see KS3 Maths Success Guide pages 82–83

AVERAGES 2

M Choose just one answer, a, b, c or d.

The following questions are based on the information given in the table below.

The weights of some potatoes:

Weight (g)	Frequency
$20 \leq W < 30$	5
$30 \leq W < 40$	6
$40 \leq W < 50$	4
$50 \leq W < 60$	5

1 How many potatoes weighed less then 50 g?
   a) 15 b) 5 c) 6 d) 20   (1 mark)

2 Which of the class intervals is the modal class?
   a) $20 \leq W < 30$ b) $30 \leq W < 40$ c) $40 \leq W < 50$
   d) $50 \leq W < 60$ (1 mark)

3 Which of the class intervals contains the median value?
   a) $20 \leq W < 30$ b) $30 \leq W < 40$ c) $40 \leq W < 50$
   d) $50 \leq W < 60$ (1 mark)

4 Estimate the mean weight of the potatoes.
   a) 39 g b) 41 g c) 39·5 g d) 43 g   (1 mark)

Score .... /4

Q Answer all parts of all questions.

1 The weights of some students in a class are measured. The results are given in the table.

Weight (kg)	Number of students
$40 \leq W < 45$	6
$45 \leq W < 50$	5
$50 \leq W < 55$	8
$55 \leq W < 60$	4
$60 \leq W < 65$	2

Explain, with justification, whether the following statements are true or false.

a) The mean weight of the students is 50·7 kg. ....

....(1 mark)

b) The modal class of the data is $55 \leq W < 60$. ....(1 mark)

c) The class interval that contains the median weight of the students is $50 \leq W < 55$.

....(1 mark)

d) Eleven students had a weight of less than 50 kg. ....(1 mark)

e) There were 20 students in total whose weight was measured. ....(1 mark)

f) The range in weights of the students was 40 kg. ....(1 mark)

Score .... /6

These are SATs-style questions. Answer all parts of the questions.

1 The frequency diagram shows the time in minutes for a group of students to do a verbal reasoning test.

a) Calculate an estimate of the mean time to do the test.

Show your working. ....minutes   (3 marks)

b) Which class interval contains the median time?..(1 mark)

A different group of students did the same verbal reasoning test. Their results are shown in the table below.

Time in minutes	Frequency (*f*)	Midpoint (*x*)	*f* × *x*
$0 \leq t < 5$	4		
$5 \leq t < 10$	18		
$10 \leq t < 15$	24		
$15 \leq t < 20$	6		
$20 \leq t < 25$	2		
$25 \leq t < 30$	1		

c) Calculate an estimate for the mean time for this group of students to do the test.

You may use the table to help you...(3 marks)

d) What is the modal class for this data?..(1 mark)

e) 'On average', which group of students did the test in a quicker time?

Justify your answer...(1 mark)

2 Mr Robinson is going to purchase some nails. He asks two companies for the following data about the length of their nails:

Company A	Company B
mean = 25 cm	mean = 25 cm
range = 8 cm	range = 1·3 cm

From which company should he purchase the nails?

Explain your reasoning.

....(2 marks)

Score .... /11

TOTAL SCORE   /21

For more help on this topic see KS3 Maths Success Guide pages 84–85

CUMULATIVE FREQUENCY GRAPHS

Q   **Answer all parts of all questions.**

1 The graph shows the number of mobile phones that a shop sold over a period of 100 days.

Estimate:

a) the median   ....

b) the lower quartile   ....

c) the upper quartile   ....

d) the interquartile range   ....

(4 marks)

2 The table shows the time in minutes for 83 people's journeys to work.

Time in minutes	Frequency	Cumulative frequency
$0 \le t < 10$	5	
$10 \le t < 20$	20	
$20 \le t < 30$	26	
$30 \le t < 40$	18	
$40 \le t < 50$	10	
$50 \le t < 60$	4	

a) Complete the cumulative frequency column in the table above. (1 mark)

b) Draw the cumulative frequency graph on the axes and grid below.

(1 mark)

c) From your graph, find the median time. ....(1 mark)

d) From your graph, find the interquartile range. ....(1 mark)

e) How many people had a journey of more than 45 minutes to work? ....(1 mark)

Score .... /9

These are SATs-style questions. Answer all parts of the questions.

1   Some students are raising money for charity. The cumulative frequency graph shows the distribution of the amount of money they raised.

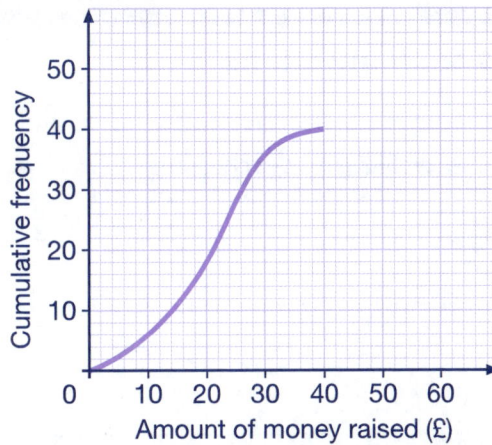

a) Read the graph to estimate the median amount of money raised. £........................(1 mark)

b) Estimate the percentage of students who raised less than £25. ....% (1 mark)

c) Using the graph, work out the value of the interquartile range.

   Interquartile range £ ....(1 mark)

Another group of students is also raising money for charity. The table shows the distribution of the amount of money raised by these students.

Money raised (£)	Cumulative frequency
< 10	4
< 20	12
< 30	22
< 40	37
< 50	45
< 60	50

d) Draw a cumulative frequency graph for these data using the axes above.   (2 marks)

e) For the graph you have just drawn:
   put a tick (✔) by any statement below which is true,
   put a cross (✗) by any statement below which is false.
   A: 25 students raised less than £32 each. ....(1 mark)
   B: The median amount raised lies between £40 and £50..(1 mark)
   C: 10% of the students raised less than £5..(1 mark)

Score .... /8

TOTAL SCORE   /17

For more help on this topic see KS3 Maths Success Guide pages 86–87

PROBABILITY 1

Q   **Answer all parts of all questions.**

1 A bag contains 3 red, 4 blue and 6 green balls. If a ball is chosen at random from the bag, what is the probability of choosing:

a) a red ball? ....(1 mark)

b) a green ball? ....(1 mark)

c) a yellow ball? ....(1 mark)

d) a blue or a red ball? ....(1 mark)

2 A box of chocolates contains 15 hard centres and 13 soft centres. One chocolate is chosen at random. Work out the probability that it will be:

a) a hard centre..(1 mark)

b) a soft centre ....(1 mark)

c) a biscuit ....(1 mark)

3 Decide whether each of these statements is true or false.

a) If the probability that I receive a letter is 72%, the probability that I do not receive a letter is 28%. ....(1 mark)

b) The probability that a flag is not coloured red is 0·26. The probability that a flag is coloured red is 0·64. ....(1 mark)

c) The probability that the 'Go Aheads' win a darts match is $\frac{41}{63}$.

The probability they do not win a darts match is $\frac{20}{63}$. ....(1 mark)

4 The probability of passing a driving test is 0·7. If 200 people take the driving test today, how many would you expect to pass?

....(1 mark)

5 Michelle is a swimmer. The probability of her winning a race is 84%. If she swims in 50 races this season, how many races would you expect her to win?

....(1 mark)

Score ...... /12

These are SATs-style questions. Answer all parts of the questions.

1   The diagram shows two spinners, Spinner X and Spinner Y.

2	3
2	4

1	3
2	3

Spinner X   Spinner Y

a) Which spinner gives you the better chance of getting a 3?
Explain your choice.

....(1 mark)

b) Which spinner gives you the better chance of obtaining an even number?
Explain your choice.

....(1 mark)

2   A box contains 50 packets of different flavoured crisps. There are four flavours – cheese, bacon, beef and tomato – in the box. The probability of choosing each flavour from the box is:

Flavour	Probability
Cheese	0·3
Bacon	0·1
Beef	....
Tomato	0·45

a) Work out the probability of choosing a beef flavoured packet of crisps.

....(1 mark)

b) Write down the most common flavour of crisps.

....(1 mark)

c) If a packet of crisps is taken at random from the box, what is the probability that it is either cheese or bacon flavour?

....(1 mark)

d) The probability that the box of crisps is damaged during transport is 42%. What is the probability that the box is not damaged?

....(1 mark)

e) 200 packets of crisps are chosen at random. Estimate the number of packets of tomato flavoured crisps in the batch of 200.

....(1 mark)

Score .... /7

TOTAL SCORE   /19

For more help on this topic see KS3 Maths Success Guide pages 88–89

PROBABILITY 2

Q **Answer all parts of all questions.**

1 A fair die is thrown 150 times. A 4 comes up 31 times.

a) What is the relative frequency of getting a 4?

....(1 mark)

b) If the number of times the die is thrown increases, what would you expect to happen to the relative frequency of obtaining a 4?

....(1 mark)

2 A fair die and a fair coin are thrown at the same time.

a) Complete the table to show the possible outcomes.

Die

		1	2	3	4	5	6
Coin	H			H3			
	T				T5		

(1 mark)

b) What is the probability of obtaining a head and a 2?

....(1 mark)

c) What is the probability of obtaining a tail and an even number?

....(1 mark)

3 Mr Smith and Mrs Tate both go to the library every Wednesday. The probability that Mr Smith takes out a fiction book is 0·8, whilst the probability that Mrs Tate takes out a fiction book is 0·4. The events are independent.

a) Complete the tree diagram by writing in the missing probabilities.

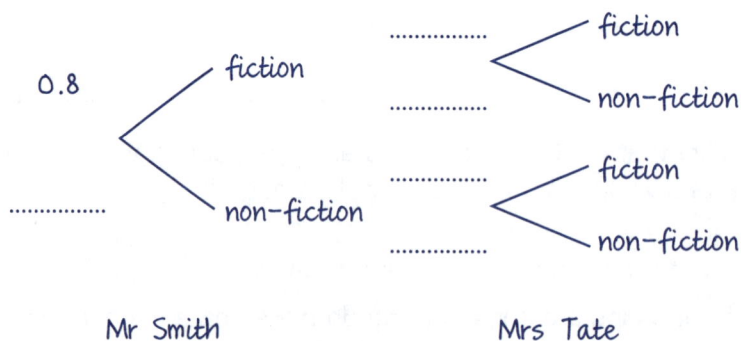

```
                              ............. ── fiction
                   fiction ──<
        0.8 ──                 ............. ── non-fiction

                              ............. ── fiction
  ............. ── non-fiction ──<
                              ............. ── non-fiction

        Mr Smith              Mrs Tate
```

(2 marks)

b) Calculate the probability that both Mr Smith and Mrs Tate take out a fiction book.

....(1 mark)

c) Calculate the probability that a fiction and a non-fiction book are taken out.

....(2 mark)

Score .... /10

88

These are SATs-style questions. Answer all parts of the questions.

1   Hywel and Tracey are playing a game. They each have four cards.

Hywel's cards are numbered:	1	3	5	7
Tracey's cards are numbered:	1	2	3	4

They each take any one of their own cards. They then multiply the numbers on the two cards.

The table shows all the possible answers:

Hywel's cards

	X	1	3	5	7
	1	1	3	5	7
Tracey's	2	2	6	10	14
cards	3	3	9	15	21
	4	4	12	20	28

a) What is the probability that their answer is a multiple of 3?

....(1 mark)

b) What is the probability that their answer is less than 12?

....(1 mark)

2   a) Melissa is a keen athlete.

She estimates that the probability she wins each race is 0·3. If she runs 20 races, how many of these races would she expect to win?

....(1 mark)

b) Simon also runs the same races.

He won 8 of the races he ran. He estimated that the probability that he wins each race is 0·4.

How many races did he run? ....(1 mark)

c) The probability that Imran wins a race is 0·6. Imran runs a race on two consecutive days. What is the probability that he will:

i) win both races? ....(1 mark)

ii) win only one of the races? ....(2 marks)

Score .... /7

TOTAL SCORE   /17

For more help on this topic see KS3 Maths Success Guide pages 90–91

Levels 5–8
Non-calculator questions.

1   The diagram shows an equilateral triangle and an isosceles triangle inside a rectangle.

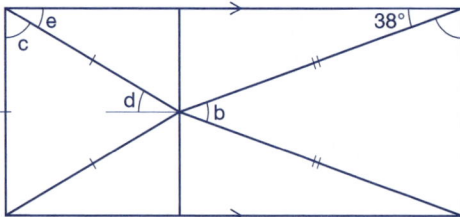

Calculate the size of the missing angles.

a = ... b = ...

c = ... d = ...

e = ...

(5 marks)

2   a) Look at these numbers:

1^4 2^3 3^4 4^2 5^3 6^1

   i)   Which is the smallest? ....**(1 mark)**

   ii) Which is equal to 2^4?...**(1 mark)**

   b) Which numbers below are square numbers?

2^3 2^4 3^5 3^4 4^6 2^7

   .... **(1 mark)**

3   a) For this sequence of numbers, 1, 4, 7, 10, …, write down the nth term of the sequence.

nth term = ... **(1 mark)**

   b) For this sequence of numbers, 1, 2, 7, 14, 23, …, write down the nth term of sequence.

nth term = ... **(1 mark)**

   c) Melissa and Javed were playing a game. Melissa said, 'Multiplying my number by 4 and adding 10 gives me an answer which is less than 30.'

   Calling Melissa's number y, form an inequality. .... **(1 mark)**

   d) Solve the inequality.   .... **(2 marks)**

   e) Javed then said:

   Melissa's number is equal to 5.

   Explain why he is wrong. ....**(1 mark)**

4   a) These are similar triangles:

Not accurately drawn

   What is the value of y?

   Show your working.   .... cm   **(1 mark)**

b)

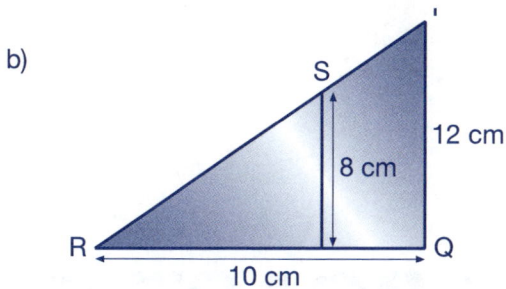

PQR and SRT are similar triangles.

What is the length of RT? .... cm **(1 mark)**

c) The diagram shows two rectangles:

Show that the two rectangles are not mathematically similar.

....

....

....

....

(1 mark)

5 At the FA Cup Final, the number of supporters who attended are given in the table below.

Football team	Number of people attended (nearest thousand)
Arsenal	32 000
Chelsea	29 000

a) Write the number of Arsenal supporters in standard form. .... **(1 mark)**

b) Write down the difference between the number of Arsenal and the number of Chelsea supporters.
Give your answer in standard form. .... **(1 mark)**

c) The number of supporters who could not get tickets for the match is approximately the same
as the product off those Arsenal and Chelsea supporters who attended the FA Cup Final.
Write down this value in standard form. ....**(1 mark)**

6 This prism is made up of two cuboids:

a) Show that the area of the cross-section of the prism is $6x^2 + 8xy$. .... **(1 mark)**

b) The volume of the prism is $4x^2(3x + 4y)$.
What is the depth of the prism?
Show your working. ....**(2 marks)**

Total: 23 marks

Levels 5–8
Calculator questions.

1   The perimeter of this shape is 3 + 2*t*.

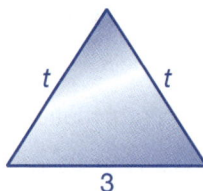

a) Write an expression for the perimeter (*p*) of each of these shapes.
   Write each expression in its simplest form.

i)

p = ... **(1 mark)**

ii)

p = ... **(1 mark)**

iii)

p = ...**(1 mark)**

b) If the perimeter of the rectangle
   below is 20 cm, calculate the value of *y*.

y = ... **(1 mark)**

2 Miss Taylor decided to organise an end-of-term trip for her class. She carried out a survey and put the results into the table below.

	Skating	Cinema	Boat trip	Bowling
Number of pupils	3	6	12	9

a) What percentage of the pupils wanted to go to the cinema? ....% **(1 mark)**

b) What fraction of the pupils wanted to go on the boat trip?

Write the fraction in its simplest form.. **(1 mark)**

c) Miss Taylor found out that the boat trip was too expensive. Out of the 12 pupils who wanted to go on the boat trip, 75% of them decided to go to the cinema Instead, whilst the remaining pupils decided to go bowling.

Complete the table below showing the number of pupils now going on each trip.

	Skating	Cinema	Bowling
Number of pupils	3	....	....

(2 marks)

d) Complete the line below to show the ratios of pupils going on each trip.

Skating : Cinema : Bowling

1 : .... : ....   **(2 marks)**

e) On the day of the trip, one of the pupils was ill and could not go. What is the probability that this pupil was going skating?

.... **(1 mark)**

3 A teacher has a pile of cards. An expression for the total number of cards is **8n + 10**.

$8n + 10$

a) The teacher makes two equal piles:

? ?

Write an expression to show the number of cards in one of the piles.

.... **(1 mark)**

b) The teacher puts all the cards together again, then she uses them to make three piles. There are 16 cards in the first pile.

16 cards — $n + 6$

First pile

$4n + 2$

Second pile

$3n + 2$

Third pile

How many cards are there in the third pile? ....(2 marks)

4 The scatter diagram shows the age of some cars and how much they are worth.

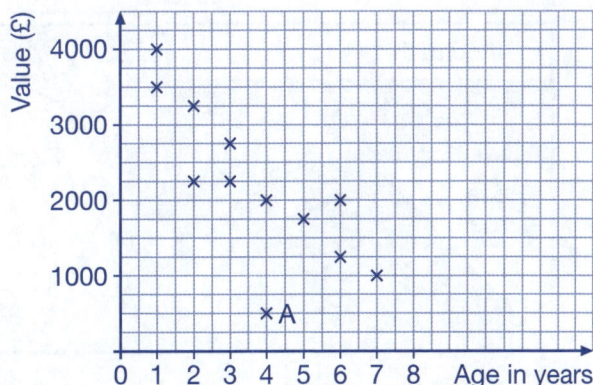

a) What does the graph show about the relationship between the age of the car and its value?

.... **(1 mark)**

b) Philip's car is 2 years old. Use the graph to estimate its value.   Value = ... **(1 mark)**

c) Car A is 4 years old but only worth £500. Explain why you think it is not worth very much.

....

.... **(1 mark)**

d) Jacqueline paid £1500 for her car. Approximately how old is it?   .... years.   **(1 mark)**

e) Draw a line of best fit on the scatter diagram.   **(1 mark)**

5 The diagram shows the graph of the straight line $y = 2x$.

a) Draw the graph of the straight line $y = 2x - 1$ **(1 mark)**

b) Draw the graph of the straight line $y = 2x + 1$.   **(1 mark)**

c) All three graphs are **parallel**. Explain which part of the equation helps you decide whether they are parallel or not.   **(1 mark)**

d) Write down the equation of another line which is parallel to $y = 2x$. $y = $ .... **(1 mark)**

e) $y = 2x$ goes through (0, 0), $y = 2x - 1$ goes through (0, -1) and $y = 2x + 1$ goes through (0, 1).

   Which part of the equation helps you see where the line crosses the y-axis?

   .... **(1 mark)**

f) Where would the line $y = 2x - 10$ cross the y-axis?

   (................. , ...)   **(1 mark)**

6 The diagram shows a plan of Emily's garden.

The garden has a fish pond, a rose garden and a footpath on the far side. The rest of the garden is grass, shown as the shaded section on the plan.

a) Calculate the area of the fish pond. Show your working.

   (Use $\pi = 3.14$.)   Area = ... m^2 **(1 mark)**

b) The area of the rose garden is 22.5 m^2.

   Calculate the perpendicular height of the rose garden.

   Show your working.   Height = ... m   **(1 mark)**

94

c) Calculate the area of ground covered by grass (the shaded section).

Show your working. Area = ... m² **(3 marks)**

d) Emily buys a shed for the garden.
Calculate the volume of the shed.
Show your working, and include the units.

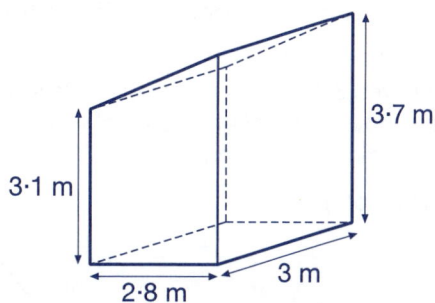

3·1 m   3·7 m   2·8 m   3 m

Volume = ... **(3 marks)**

e) Emily plants red and white rose trees in the rose garden in the ratio 2 : 3.

If she plants 40 trees in total, how many are white?   White roses = ... **(1 mark)**

7 Imran's class did a multiplication tables test. There were 50 questions in the test.
The results are shown in the table below:

Number of correct answers	Number of pupils (*f*)	Midpoint of group (*x*)	*f x*
1–10	3		
11–20	8		
21–30	5		
31–40	10		
41–50	6		

a) Calculate an estimate of the mean number of marks achieved in the test. Show your working.
You may complete the table above to help you with the calculation.

Mean = ... **(2 marks)**

Two other Year 9 classes did the same tables test.
Their results are shown in the table below.

	Average	Range
9A	24	24
9B	32	4

After looking at the results, Imran said: '9B did better than 9A in the tables test.'

b) Explain why this may not be true. .... **(1 mark)**

8 Charlotte decides to go for a walk. She leaves her home at 0930 hours and walks at a speed of 5 km/h.
She arrives at the lake at 1130 hours. She then walks to her friend's house at an average speed of
4 km/h. It takes her 1½ hours to walk to her friend's house.

Sunnymead
Lake

Charlotte's
friend's house

Charlotte's
house

not drawn to scale

a) How far is the lake from Charlotte's house?   .... km   **(1 mark)**

b) How far does Charlotte's friend live from the lake? .... km **(1 mark)**

c) The lake is due North of Charlotte's house and her friend lives due East of the lake.
   Calculate the shortest distance between Charlotte's house and her friend's house.

   .... km **(2 marks)**

d) Charlotte's aunt lives 3 km away from Charlotte's house.
   On the diagram above and using a scale of 1 cm = 2 km, shade in all the possible
   areas in which Charlotte's aunt can live. **(2 marks)**

9 a) Calculate the value of p.

25

42°

p

Show your working. $p =$ .... **(2 marks)**

b) Calculate the value of angle n.

24 cm

37 cm

n

Show your working. $n =$ .... **(2 marks)**

10 The information in the table shows the time customers spent queuing at a supermarket checkout.

Time (t minutes)	Frequency	Cumulative frequency
$0 \le t < 2$	4	
$2 \le t < 4$	12	
$4 \le t < 6$	20	
$6 \le t < 8$	10	
$8 \le t < 10$	4	

a) On the table above complete the cumulative frequency column. **(1 mark)**

b) On the grid below, draw the cumulative frequency graph.

(2 marks)

c) Using your graph, estimate the median waiting time. Median = ... **(1 mark)**

d) Using your graph, estimate the interquartile range.

Interquartile range = ... **(2 marks)**

Total: 53 marks